SECRET SOCIETIES IN DETROIT

BILL LOOMIS

THE
History
PRESS

Published by The History Press
Charleston, SC
www.historypress.com

Copyright © 2021 by William Loomis
All rights reserved

First published 2021

Manufactured in the United States

ISBN 9781467146524

Library of Congress Control Number: 2020944167

CONTENTS

CONTENTS

INTRODUCTION

In years past, being alone meant something different than today. If you lived alone on the Detroit River in 1850, at night, you sat in your small house with no sounds except those made by nature: the water sounds of the river, the cow in the cow cabin, ducks crossing the night sky, the wind in the trees. A little light from a fireplace, a candle or a kerosene lamp barely held back the darkness. Night after night after night—a lifetime spent against the great silence. This was not in some remote corner of the state but even as close as a few miles down the road from Detroit. The daily experience of being alone.

We have nothing like that today. I doubt one could find a spot in the United States that doesn't have the sound of automobile tires lashing pavement, let alone aircraft thousands of feet above. With phones and the internet, we live in constant noise. But it's not hard to imagine a driving need of people in the nineteenth century to be around others. People were lonely. They literally got cabin fever. They joined with people to escape silence.

A column that ran twice weekly in the *Detroit Free Press* in 1919 was titled Are Men Lonelier Than Women? Women and men would write in to the editor of the lonely column complaining of how hard it was to meet people or providing tips on how to lose loneliness, which were not very good. These included: "Have a smile for everyone you meet, and they will have a smile for you" or "I can honestly assure anyone that they need never have a reason to regret having known me." But there was one suggestion I thought was good. On May 3, 1919, a woman wrote: "One way to remedy this condition would be the formation of clubs, to which both men and women could belong."

People loved belonging to clubs for reasons that ranged from fun and laughs to saving America from something evil. They stood shoulder to shoulder to work for a shared moral good. They belonged to a gang to commit horrible crimes with childhood friends. Many times, it was something mundane, such as pooling resources to provide life insurance or retirement income. Sometimes it was for self-improvement.

There was (and is) a common xenophobic response by some Americans whenever there is a significant increase in immigration by a specific group to the United States or a population shift from one area to another, such as in Detroit. Some believed these masses of immigrants were an existential threat "to my country, my church, my heritage and my life," so these threatened people mocked and battled the immigrants relentlessly and viciously. A dark side of "taking care of your own" seems to mean taking the law into your own hands by some.

In 1992, American historian Robert V. Remini wrote in the *New York Times*, "An ugly frightening streak runs through the entire course of this nation's history, and Americans need to remind themselves regularly of its lurking presence lest they forget that organized bigotry is not a foreign contagion. It is as American as violence, capitalism and democracy."

Clubs and cults reflected the nineteenth century's confidence in the power of group activity to accomplish goals and change the world. In the 1840s, French philosopher Charles Fourier became popular across the United States. Fourier declared that concern and cooperation were the secrets of social success. He believed that a society that cooperated would see an immense improvement in its productivity levels. The word *association* was Fourieristic terminology that began to be used in the 1840s. In the ritual of the secret society called the Union League during the Civil War, the league's president was instructed to "increase the membership, for it is only by association we can expect to succeed."

Likewise, the word *organization* is a term made popular in the pseudomedical practice of phrenology. To the phrenologist, the brain was composed of "organs," and their arrangement was called "organ-ization" which could in part determine your character. This was popularly applied in the nineteenth century to the optimal arrangement of people in groups.

Many, if not most, of the clubs were secret, requiring passwords, secret handshakes, symbols and guarded meetings closed to the public because people, men mostly, loved belonging to a secret, exclusive group. Sometimes secrecy was much more serious. Secret clubs were formed during wartimes, like the Civil War or World War II, out of real fear and distrust of strangers and even neighbors. Just belonging to the club could be considered treason. Saying the wrong thing to the wrong person could get you hanged.

Part of the interest in researching and writing about clubs and cults is the creators of many of these groups or secret societies, like George Bickley, Justus Henry Rathbone or even Detroit's own Donald Lobsinger. For these men, new clubs were a way to make a fortune, to build friendships or to hold back a rising tide of evil against a naïve public.

Not all of the groups in this book began in Detroit. Several were national movements that also found a home in Detroit and made an impact. Some causes were noble, but too many were despicable. Courage and virtuous behavior for noble causes lasted much longer than "great" acts for low causes. Followers were seldom as committed or willing to make sacrifices as leaders believed; in most cases, the followers either didn't exist or were no-shows.

In any case, these groups were a way many people dealt with the world in the past and are an aspect of human nature worthy of revisiting.

We are and should be interested in how any man solves his problems and acquits himself in his battles.
—*F.L. Mott*

PART I.

BEFORE THE CIVIL WAR

1

MASONS FROM THE START

The Order of Free and Accepted Masons is very old. No one is sure of its beginning, but documents in Europe connected to the group have been dated to 1390. It began as an ancient guild of stonemasons who built medieval churches, chapels, cathedrals, monasteries and more. It was and always has been a secret society. Many of its mysterious symbols, hand grips and signs are claimed to be rooted in the medieval masons' values: the symbols of a compass, level and arch, for instance. Because the masons worked independently of the church and moved about from one job to another, they were referred to as the "free" masons. While considered sinister by some, their stated mission has always been benign: "Make good men better."

And today's Masonic lodges in the United States have a largely harmless image, seen as a place for small-town businessmen (the order is limited to men; women belong to the Eastern Stars) to engage in social gatherings, networking and opportunities for charity. But the group was not always so harmless.

It is a group that might seem to be a humble union of craftsmen, but its influence in Europe, North America and even Detroit was powerful and was feared and hated by some, such as the Catholic Church. The United States Masons (also known as Freemasons) originated in England and became a popular association for leading colonials after the first American lodge was founded in Boston in 1733. Masonic brothers pledged to support one another and provide sanctuary if needed.

Fourteen U.S. presidents have been Masons, starting with George Washington. President Gerald Ford was initiated on September 30, 1949, in Malta Lodge No. 465 in Grand Rapids. The masons attracted the elite of society, and their influence was once immense. Take out a U.S. dollar bill and look at the back. On the left side, across from the eagle on the right, is a seeing eye and a pyramid. What is that? The eye above the pyramid is a Masonic symbol. In Masonic lore, the pyramid symbol is referred to as the eye of God watching over humanity.

Some scholars say as many as twenty-one signers of the Declaration of Independence were Masons. Many historians note that the Constitution and the Bill of Rights both seem to be heavily influenced by the Masonic "civic religion," which focuses on freedom, free enterprise and a limited role for the state.

But the secretive club was always under suspicion from those who saw the Masons as elite and scheming.

THE HISTORY OF THE MASONS AND THE CITY OF DETROIT GO HAND IN HAND FROM THE START

In 1758, François-Marie Picoté, sieur de Belestre (November 17, 1716–March 30, 1793), became the thirteenth and last official French commandant of Fort Ponchartrain in Detroit. De Belestre was a practicing Mason in Montreal, and Masons claimed that freemasonry was common in French-founded cities and outposts.

Detroit's first Masonic lodge was established by the British, who took control of Detroit in 1760, and it is claimed that Detroit's was the oldest Masonic lodge west of the Allegheny Mountains. It was founded only thirty years after the very first lodge in North America. (A Masonic lodge is the basic organizational unit of the Masons. Lodges are started with a charter issued by the state grand lodge.) That first Detroit lodge was founded by Lieutenant John Christie of the Second Battalion, Sixtieth Royal American Foot Regiment ("Royal Americans"), on April 27, 1764. It was named the Zion Lodge No. 10 and was chartered by the Grand Lodge in New York. Most soldiers at the time were British born, but the Royal Americans were recruited along the banks of the Hudson River between New York City and Albany. Many of the Americans were Masons, so they petitioned to the grand lodge to form a lodge and confer degrees. At the time, there were about two thousand inhabitants in Detroit and three hundred buildings. The Masons met in a guardhouse of the fort. An additional four lodges

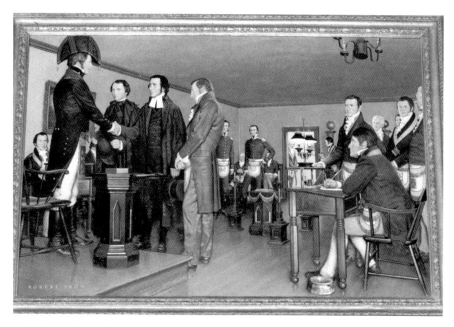

A 1967 painting by Robert A. Thom showing the Masons presenting the money to fund the University of Michigan, originally called the Catholepistemiad, or the University of Michigania. The term *Catholepitemiad* had nothing to do with the Catholic Church but was used by Augustus B. Woodward, who started the idea of the university. The Masonic Foundation of the Grand Lodge of Free and Accepted Masons of Michigan gifted the painting *The Founding of the University of Michigan* to the university in November 1967. *Bentley Historical Library, University of Michigan.*

were chartered over the next twenty years, and meetings were held in men's homes. A notice of a meeting from one of the lodges read as follows:

> *Detroit 23rd August, 1799*
> *Brother May—*
>   *You are requested to meet the master Wardens and the rest of the Brethren at the house of James Donaldson on the 33rd of Aug, immediately at 6 o'clock in the evening, being a Lodge of Emergency, and this you are to accept as special summons from Zion Lodge no. 10 of the Registry of Lower Canada. Fail not on your O.B.*
> *By Order of the Body,*
> *Ben. Rand, Secretary of Zion Lodge*

Locally, of $3,000 in seed money raised to start the University of Michigan in 1817, $2,100 came from Masonic Lodge Zion Lodge No. 62 and from individual Freemasons. Opened in Detroit in 1817, the school moved to Ann Arbor in 1837.

Detroit membership grew steadily. Masons love hierarchy and ranks. The senior officer of a Masonic lodge is the master, normally addressed and referred to as the "Worshipful Master." The worshipful master sits on the east of the lodge room, chairs all of the business of his lodge and is vested with considerable powers. He also presides over ritual and ceremonies. Lodges also have senior and junior wardens, a secretary, a treasurer, a deacon, a steward and a tiler (who guards the outer door from intruders). Grand lodges preside over the state and grant charters for new lodges. They are headed by grand master masons. Detroit's very first grand master mason was Lewis Cass.

Each ranking officer has individual "jewels" signifying his position, as well as velvet collars, chains and more. In addition, members carried ceremonial swords, short officer aprons, gavels, the Bible, rods and clothing for candidates. All Masons wore white gloves, aprons, shirts, hats, caps, breast jewels and a variety of rings, pins and watches. All of this is referred to as "regalia."

Even though Masons were secretive, they loved to march in parades through the city streets. This comment on a parade in Philadelphia in 1851 was typical of the times: "The number of Masons in this procession was about eighteen hundred, and a finer looking and more respectable body of men was never seen in any public parade in this city.…The Grand Officers in full regalia were on the right, followed by officers and members of the blue lodges attired in white aprons and blue scarves."

THE RISE OF THE ANTI-MASONS

In 1826, the anti-masonic movement emerged in western New York state and spread to Detroit. The anti-masonic movement strongly opposed Freemasonry, believing it to be a corrupt and elitist closed society secretly ruling much of the country in defiance of American principles. The anti-masonic party was founded in 1828, in the aftermath of the disappearance of William Morgan, a bricklayer and former Mason from Batavia, New York, who had become a prominent critic of the Masonic organization and threatened to reveal its secrets. Many believed an unfounded conspiracy that the Masons abducted and murdered Morgan for speaking out against Masonry. Subsequently, many churches and other groups condemned Masonry. Some Masons were prominent businessmen and politicians, so the backlash against the Masons was also a form of anti-elitism. The anti-

A published illustration showing the alleged abduction of Morgan. Suspicion of Freemasonry was so pervasive that the Anti-Mason Party became a third political party during the presidency of John Quincy Adams. *Public domain.*

masonic political party became the first third party in the United States during John Quincy Adams's presidency.

It was said that people who moved to the Michigan Territory in the late 1820s and 1830s from counties in western New York, where William Morgan was from, brought the anti-masonic movement to Michigan and Detroit. In Detroit, the anger fomented by the anti-masons toward Masons pitted neighbors against neighbors and was said to split families. Masons in villages like Stoney Creek in Oakland County were driven from their churches.

Anti-Mason Judge Samuel W. Dexter

Samuel William Dexter arrived in Detroit from western New York in 1824. A Harvard graduate and a practicing lawyer, Dexter came from a prominent eastern family. (His father was a U.S. senator, secretary of war under Adams and secretary of the treasury under Jefferson.)

Dexter chose to settle on the Michigan frontier. He arrived with $80,000 and spent the first four months exploring southern Michigan, traveling on horseback. He proceeded to purchase 926 acres of land in Michigan. On that land, Dexter founded Byron, Michigan (named after the poet), and Saginaw. He also purchased land in Webster and Scio Townships in Washtenaw County, on which he later founded the village of Dexter. He built a sawmill and a gristmill on Mill Creek and a log cabin nearby. Dexter returned to Massachusetts in 1825 and married his second wife, Susan Dunham. He was appointed the village of Dexter's first postmaster, and in 1826, when Washtenaw was formally organized as a county, he was chosen as its first chief justice. From then on, he was always referred to as Judge Dexter. He claimed that the village of Dexter was named after his father.

He was a temperate man and rigidly opposed to oathbound secret societies, such as the Masons. Along with the founder of Ann Arbor, John Allen, in 1829, Dexter began an anti-masonic newspaper, the *Ann Arbor Emigrant*. It was the first newspaper in Washtenaw County. Together the two men made Washtenaw County a hotbed of anti-masonic politics. In 1831, the *Ann Arbor Emigrant* published, "Masons have taken such and such obligations upon themselves therefore I will denounce them as a set of cut-throats, perjurers and traitors till they come out and secede from masonry."

In 1829, fearful of angry mobs, Grand Master Lewis Cass ordered the grand lodge and advised all subordinate lodges in Michigan to suspend their activity. This continued for eleven years as the wave of antipathy toward Freemasonry swept across Michigan and the rest of the world. With the reelection of Andrew Jackson, a well-known grand master mason, anti-masons lost faith in the cause and their political party and joined the Whigs. By 1840, the anti-masons had been forgotten.

Freemasonry continued to reorganize and grow in Detroit as the following lodges were chartered: Union Lodge of Strict Observance (1852), Ashlar Lodge (1857), Oriental Lodge (1868), Schiller Lodge (1869) and Kilwinning Lodge (1872).

Another boost to their popularity came in early June 1870, when the Knights Templar, a branch of the Freemasons, arrived from across the country to hold its national convocation and march for its "grand review." It was nearly one thousand strong, in uniform, walking down the streets of Detroit, as reported in the *Detroit Free Press* on June 19, 1870:

> By eleven o'clock every knightly body was on the ground with eight bands of music to thrill the pulses of the thousands of spectators who lined both walks of the avenue from end to end. Dressed alike, their uniforms rich but not gaudy, their white plumes nodding in the morning breeze, their swords

gleaming in the sunshine, and the gallant knights made such a parade as was never before witnessed in Detroit. Up they marched, stepping to the beat of the drums, looking like the knights of olden times. Wherever the head of the tramping column turned, its vision was greeted with flags and banners—waving from staffs, fluttering from windows, held in the hands of ladies, flung across the street, giving the city a holiday appearance.

By the prosperous 1920s, Masonry in Detroit had hit its highest popularity. Gone was much of the quasi-religious costume and ceremony of the nineteenth century. It still maintained its elaborate rituals to promote a sense of exclusivity, but now it grew more secular to accommodate the American value of enterprise. In Detroit, about half the membership of Freemasonry was made up of lower-class white-collar managers who were generally Protestant. This included the assembly line plant foremen. Foremen are plant management's enforcers. While they were technically part of management and not assembly line workers, they dressed like workers and had no office or phone, though some stood at small podiums off to the side of the assembly line to do minor paperwork. They were paid more than line workers and considered themselves socially above hourly workers. Masonry promoted brotherhood, respectability and sober self-improvement to get ahead in your career. It stood for unqualified Americanism. Importantly, it distinguished native-born Protestant foremen from the line workers who were generally Catholics, uneducated and from an ethnic group, such as German or Polish. Foremen proudly displayed their Masonic rings. Masonry also provided another social communication network among fellow foremen, which gave a buffer to hierarchical dictates from upper management.

As quoted in the book *On the Line, Essays in the History of Auto Work*, from Ford foundry foreman Roy Campbell remembering the mid-1930s, "If you wanted to get anyplace or hold a job with any responsibility you better be a Mason." This was pervasive with supervisory employees throughout Detroit plants.

THE GREAT FOLLOWED BY THE GREATEST

Masons continued to add members and build larger Masonic temples. In 1851, the Masons built a brick building at Griswold and Shelby. In 1876, they leased a larger building on Jefferson Avenue. In 1893, they opened what at the time was considered an enormous temple—six stories high and described as a "magnificent addition to the city" by the *Detroit Free Press*.

Detroit's Masonic temple. *Public domain.*

The main entrance was on Lafayette Boulevard. It had a stone façade in the Romanesque style of the times.

However, by the spring of 1919, Detroit had sixty lodges and forty thousand members who were struggling with the cramped quarters at the Lafayette Boulevard temple. A meeting was held with representatives from all of the Detroit lodges at the Detroit Athletic Club. It was decided that they would build a new temple at the cost of $2 million. The money would not be raised with bonds but through subscriptions from individual members; a competition was started among the lodges to see who could bring in the most money. The nationally famous architect George D. Mason was selected for the project.

The fundraising campaign spread nationwide as donations came in from Masons across the country, and the $2 million was raised from additional funds to $4 million. With the money in hand, George Mason submitted his designs for what would eventually be the largest masonic temple in the world, located across from Cass Park. (Chicago's Masonic temple was the largest until 1939, when it was destroyed by fire, making Detroit the largest.)

The groundbreaking ceremony was set for Thanksgiving Day, November 25, 1920. On a cold and cloudy day, twenty thousand Masons marched in the Thanksgiving Day parade wearing their famous white gloves and white aprons, row after row stretching curb to curb across Woodward Avenue and up to Bagg Street (now Temple Avenue), the future site of the temple. There Masons and their families gathered for the "turning of the sod" ceremony.

The cornerstone was laid on September 18, 1922, a ceremony attended again by tens of thousands of Detroiters. For the ceremony, a trowel was used that once belonged to George Washington, a master Mason, during the construction of the U.S. Capitol. The event was attended by President Warren G. Harding, who spoke at the event.

The building was completed in 1926. George Mason's unique design was neo-Gothic, using lots of Indiana limestone. It was a style he believed exemplified Masons and their traditions. Included in the massive building are three theaters. One was never completed and is referred to as the "unfinished theater." Another theater, previously the Scottish Ritual Theater, is now the Jack White Theater, named after Detroit native and rock star Jack White, who generously saved the temple from foreclosure in April 2013 by paying $142,000 in county back taxes. The Masons had helped White's mother when she was out of work and in need by giving her a job as an usher at the theater.

The building also includes a Shrine building, the chapel, eight lodge rooms, a 17,500-square-foot drill hall (now used for roller derby), two ballrooms, office space, a cafeteria, dining rooms, a swimming pool, a gymnasium, a barbershop and sixteen bowling lanes—1,037 rooms in total.

George Mason also incorporated the artistic conceptions of the sculptor Corrado Parducci, an artist well known in Detroit because of his stone sculptures and embellishments in buildings throughout the city. The building's lobby, designed by Parducci, was an adaptation of the interior of a castle he had visited in Palermo, Sicily. Parducci also designed light fixtures and chandeliers, decorative arches, medallions, plaster decorations and other artistic details throughout the building.

In a 1975 interview with Smithsonian historian Dennis Barrie, Parducci discussed the interior of the immense building. "Now all the interior of the Masonic Temple....I better talk about that to you because that's kind of interesting. There are about a dozen large rooms, very large, you know, lodges, and every one is a different style. There's a Greek....The ballroom is Renaissance, and there's a cathedral in there which is Gothic, and then there's some Tudor rooms, there's an Egyptian room, and there's the Doric room....Now all these rooms are in the character and style of a particular period! And I had them all on my fingertips."

2

THE HUNTER'S LODGES AND THE DETROIT INVASION OF CANADA

Hunter's Lodges were started in American cities along the Canadian border from Vermont to Michigan in military support of a rebellion in Canada to overthrow the British colonizers and develop a self-governing republic. The rebellion was called the Patriot War. It lasted from 1837 to 1838 and had support of French Canadians and immigrant Irish who felt the British governing was harsh and excluded them.

Detroit's Hunter's Lodge was run by Henry C. Handy. While passionate about the cause to overthrow the British, most lodges were made of young, inexperienced farmers and businessmen who were easily defeated by seasoned British troops and disciplined Canadian militias. The "war" was short-lived, and Detroit's attack on Windsor was the final battle of the event. The cause was popular, and the thought of courageous fighting and glory of victory excited the imaginations of a generation of Americans whose fathers had fought in the War of 1812 or the American Revolution. Michigan's first governor, Stevens T. Mason, was said to be a member of a Hunter's Lodge. There was a representative branch of the Hunter's Lodge in Washington, D.C., and President Martin Van Buren was sympathetic to the cause.

Detroit's Hunter's Lodge was important, a "grand lodge," and Henry C. Handy, as commander and chief, was better than most of the Hunter leaders. He organized the Patriot Army of the Northwest and developed a network of spies and armed insurgents that was said to number twenty thousand, although exaggerated numbers were common. He armed these men starting in 1837 by raiding state and county jails and stealing muskets and ammunition, and when more muskets were needed, Handy made plans to raid much bigger U.S. arsenals, the closest being in Dearborn.

When fully armed, Handy's plan was to attack southwestern Ontario, then called Upper Canada and islands, such as Pelee Island along Lake Erie and the village of Windsor, which had only three hundred citizens, no British regular troops, a couple hundred volunteer militiamen, a company of fugitive American slaves and some Native warriors. The Windsor defenders had no cannon and limited arms. Veteran British soldiers were stationed in Lower Canada, near Quebec. (In 1791, Canada was divided into two provinces: Lower and Upper Canada. Lower Canada was east of Ontario, and Upper Canada was Ontario.)

The Detroit Hunter's Lodge met at the Eagle Tavern at 69 Woodbridge, and one veteran of those days recalled nights with "long inflammatory speeches that went far into the night," but the Eagle proprietor, Horace Heath, "would freely spread his well laden table for his Hunter brethren, receiving only what they were willing and able to pay."

The lodges were modeled on the Masons, with strict secrecy, dark and frightening oaths and four degrees of rank: Snowshoe, Beaver, Grand Hunter and Patriot Hunter. The sign of the Beaver was made by one person asking, "Do you know the beaver to be an industrious animal?" The response to this question was to place your thumb, nail up, between your teeth and your fingers curled beneath your chin to imitate a beaver gnawing a tree. While some shady members were in it to plunder Canadian farms, many Hunters were businessmen and leaders in the community. Most were young unemployed men; the average age was twenty-four, with some as young as sixteen. The 1830s endured some severe economic depressions, adding to the instability of the times, and drew men with free time to the cause.

The first meeting was held in Detroit's city hall, and taking a prominent part was a Detroiter named Dr. Edward Alexander Theller. Dr. Theller was described as "plump, full figured, black haired, with blue eyes, straight, well-formed nose with a high forehead, and about five feet six inches in height." He was born in Ireland in 1804 and educated in an English college, where he distinguished himself as a linguist. He acquired Latin, Greek, Spanish, and French of which he was fluent in all. In 1824, he immigrated to Montreal, where he practiced medicine for several years. During the cholera epidemic in 1832, Theller made his way to Detroit, where he was one of the city's most active physicians. He eventually opened wholesale groceries and apothecaries at 119 Jefferson Avenue, another at 27 Atwater Street, and a third at 140 Larned. Theller was appointed a brigadier general and charged with command of the first French and Irish troops that would be raised from uprisings in Canada.

Handy had the next meeting held in a Detroit theater, where there was great enthusiasm for the Canadian cause. All money and arms collected were dedicated to the Hunter's Lodge and the Patriots. Four days later, the Patriots stole fifty muskets from the city jail. Things were heating up. The Patriots had become so outrageous in their plans and threats that Governor Mason quietly asked them to move out of Detroit. Handy agreed. They would resettle in Gibraltar, twenty miles downriver and across from the Canadian Fort Malden. The steamboat *Macomb* and schooner *Ann* were secured to move men and arms; however, General Hugh Brady and the Brady Guards representing the United States to protect national neutrality took control of the arms and threatened to arrest any on Gibraltar.

The Canadians in Windsor had nothing to protect themselves, neither men nor weapons nor any provisions. They had two small militias and some volunteers. The city magistrates met and decided they would use the city's two ferries to guard the shoreline, but they had no money to buy weapons for the militias and volunteers. One magistrate, James Dougall, was a grocer and wholesaler. He had a large sum of money set aside in the Michigan Bank in Detroit, ready to send to England to buy his spring goods. He used that money through a contact in Detroit, who purchased the muskets and ammunition to be boxed up and sent on the earliest boat to Windsor. The magistrates sent over two rowboats, but as they were loading the rifles onto the boats, Dr. Theller and about one hundred Hunters got wind of the plot and charged down on them as they shoved off, rowing madly. Theller and the others didn't have time to arm themselves, so all they could do was chuck cord wood at the boats as they rowed off.

On January 6, 1838, Theller and others seized the schooner *Ann*, which was docked in Detroit, and loaded it with more stolen muskets and a small brass cannon to take to Gibraltar.

While citizens of Detroit openly favored the Patriots, worried government officials met to figure out ways to preserve U.S. neutrality in the affairs. Michigan governor Stevens T. Mason led two hundred Michigan militia on two steamers to arrest the rebels and prevent breaches in international peace, but it was said that Mason was friendly with the rebelling Patriots and simply sailed around all night and came back emptyhanded.

There was much excitement on the Canadian side. The Canadians sent the steamer *Alliance* with two hundred newly armed troops with those rifles purchased in Detroit to seize the *Ann*. They found it fourteen miles south, moored at Fort Malden in front of the city of Amherstburg, shelling the city with the small six-pounder brass cannon.

That night, Canadians disembarked on Bois Blanc Island directly across from Amherstburg. They hid behind trees about 1,500 feet from the *Ann*. The next day, the *Ann* cut its moorings and began to tack toward Bois Blanc to get to Gibralter when the Canadian soldiers began a "galling fire" on the schooner. Several men on the *Ann* were shot, and the halyards were cut down by the gunfire, dropping the mainsail and leaving the *Ann* powerless. Theller and the Patriots retreated to the ship's hold to hide from the muskets that were firing without cease from point-blank range.

Soon the Canadians boarded the *Ann*, and the Americans surrendered. Also helping capture the *Ann* was the Second Essex Company of Coloured Volunteers, who manned Fort Malden. They were refugee U.S. slaves living in Amherstburg. Theller was the only man wearing a uniform, along with a large gilt star, so he was called out by name and arrested as the leader. He turned over his pistols and sword and had to swim with the others among the ice on the Detroit River to Fort Malden.

He was transferred to Toronto, where he was to be hanged, but his wife and a contingent of Irish Canadians intervened, and his sentence was lowered to prison in the citadel—the impregnable Queen Victoria fortress in Quebec. Theller and three others were locked in a heavily guarded gun room with two small windows covered by thick iron bars.

The four Detroiters arrived at the fort in Quebec in June but after two months decided they would try to escape. There were friends and sympathizers on the outside who provided tools. Among the Americans locked up was a boy who was *Ann*'s fifer, so along with the tools, the prisoners also got a fife that the boy played, and others danced to drown out the sound of the saws cutting through the iron bars. Theller was a master at distracting the guards with conversations about London and homesickness over glasses of porter. The plan was to climb out of the small window, lower down the stone wall to the grounds and then climb a twelve-foot board fence to get to the city. They needed a night of heavy rain because the sentries neglected their rounds in the rain. Finally, in October, they got their downpour. Theller managed to drug the guards' porter with laudanum, and they made their break—the fifer boy, Colonel Dodge, a man named Parker and Theller. Theller had to remove his coat to squeeze through the small window but still managed to get wedged for a few panicked moments. He finally freed himself, slid down a rope made of bedsheets and, with his coat in his teeth, climbed up and over the fence.

They had instructions on where to hide in the city. When the prison realized they had escaped, an all-out manhunt began, with British soldiers checking every possibility, including opening coffins, but after several days, the Americans remained undiscovered. Eventually, they were hidden on a boat and carried across the St. Lawrence River to New York and safety. Theller and the others returned as heroes to Detroit one day before the final deadly fiasco—an attack on Windsor by the Hunter's Lodge.

Hunter's Lodges from Ohio and Pennsylvania joined Hunter's Lodge men in Buffalo and Rochester, New York. One hundred men from the County of Monroe, Michigan, and others from Detroit, encamped at the Swan River near Monroe. Some moved on north of Detroit, to the woods at the old Bloody Run site. In all, there were 362 impatient young men whose blood was up, eager for action. Their commander was Major General Bierce, who tried to keep things under control. They marched to Detroit for a steamer that was to take them to Windsor, but Bierce claimed the steamer was not ready and marched them back to the woods. Bierce said that he was waiting for recruits from the South to join them, but by now, the young soldiers were mutinous and began leaving. Bierce was finally roused to make a move and said if they were so ready to die, he would lead them to Windsor, but by this time, the Canadians knew they were coming. There were now only 240 men.

At 3:00 a.m. on December 4, 1838, they marched through the streets of Detroit to the river pier and took command of the steamer *Champlain* and were soon on the shores of Canada. They burned the soldiers' barracks in Windsor and a paddle steamer named the *Thames* as what was described as a "howling mob" of five thousand Detroiters cheered them on from Atwater Street and the flames rose. Young boys ran to the riverbanks to dig out cannonballs fired by the Canadian militia that bounced and rolled on the ice and stuck in the icy banks on the Detroit side. The Americans also killed and mutilated the body of a well-respected doctor, Dr. Hume, which infuriated the British leader of the Essex County militia, Colonel John C. Prince. The militia was soon joined by forty to fifty mounted Indians and began driving the Hunters back to an orchard four miles north of Windsor. General Bierce called a retreat, but the Hunters soon realized that their steamer, *Champlain*, was no longer there. Mass confusion ensued as men battled for canoes to paddle back to Detroit. The county militia set up cannon and fired at the canoe paddlers. One Hunter, Captain James Armstrong of Port Huron, was hit by cannon fire as he reached Belle Isle, which mutilated his arm. He was taken to a doctor in Detroit, where his arm was amputated. According the Detroit historian Friend Palmer, Armstrong never muttered a groan during the operation, which was done without anesthetic, but when it was finished, he picked up the arm and waved it over his head shouting, "Hurrah for the Patriots! I'm willing to lose another arm for the cause."

Twenty-five of the Hunters were killed, and forty-six were taken prisoner. Of the twenty-five killed, four were executed on the spot by the enraged British colonel Prince. Many others would have suffered the same fate if county militia officers had not checked Prince's "inhuman rashness," as it was described.

The Battle of Windsor ended the Patriot War and the passionate cause of the Hunter's Lodges, but the excitement of the war continued for many months along the shores of both sides of the river. Canada kept its militia on guard for long after. When one squad of the company would relieve the other at night or in the morning, they would discharge their muskets, waking residents in Windsor and Detroit. It reminded the inhabitants that "eternal vigilance is the price of liberty."

3

THE KNOW-NOTHINGS
IN DETROIT

The neophyte finds himself in the ante-chamber of the Know Nothings.
[He is] then told to hold up his right hand and answer the following:
Are you in religious belief a Roman Catholic?
Were your parents or grandparents born in this country?
Did either your parents or grandparents participate in the War of Independence
in 1776 on behalf of the United States?
Are you willing to support for offices of trust or profit native-born Americans
in preference to foreigners, Roman Catholics in particular?
—Excerpt of the initiation ritual of the Know-Nothings, Detroit Free Press,
August 23, 1854

Immigration to the United States before 1840 did little to alarm established Americans. People came at about 10,000 per year, and by 1840, 600,000 people had immigrated, which was about 3.0 percent of the U.S. population (17 million) at that time. From 1840 until 1850 (mostly in the latter half of the decade), 1.7 million immigrants arrived, about 7.0 percent of the population. By 1850, 9.7 percent of the United States population were foreign born. What really alarmed people was the percentage of Catholics who were immigrating. Nearly one-third of all immigrants from 1830 until 1840 were Irish Catholics, and one half of the 1.7 million immigrants in the next decade were Irish. By the end of 1860, three-fifths of all immigrants were Catholic. This was now considered a political danger.

Anti-Catholic sentiment and hatred of the pope originated before the start of the United States and could probably be traced to England, where Catholics of the time were "not entitled to toleration." The American colonists had French Catholic enemies to the north and Spanish Catholic enemies in the west. The fiery vituperation and hatred came from Protestant preachers, such as Lyman Beecher, starting in the 1830s at the Hanover Street Congregational Church in Boston, with hellfire oration that consumed the "whoredom of Babylon" and the "foul beast of Roman Catholicism." With his son Edward at another Boston Church, the Beechers fed the hatred with sermons about the "the Pope, the anti-Christ, corrupt monks, immoral nuns," and "the dirty ignorant Irish and German immigrants" who "guzzled beer and whiskey" and "who stole bread from the mouths of honest Anglo Saxon mechanics [workingmen]." The churches were soon packed every Sunday. Sermons became more lurid, describing convents as "priest's brothels" and claiming that their illegitimate infants were strangled and secretly buried in underground catacombs. Soon street mobs burned a convent in Charlestown, near Boston.

The anti-Catholic movement was called nativism, and Anglo-Saxon members were called, ironically, Native Americans—Americans born in America by American parents. They came from low levels of society and started in New York City slums, ramrodding their candidates to victory with ballot stuffing, extreme violence, riots and mob intimidation and spread-eagle yelling patriotism, making moderate opponents seem weak and uncertain. The most notorious was William Poole, known on the street as "Bill the Butcher."

This was happening in the crowded eastern cities, such as New York, Boston and Philadelphia, but what about the old Northwest, including Ohio, Indiana, Illinois, Wisconsin, part of Minnesota and Michigan? In the 1830s and 1840s, this area was primarily vacant federal land, 230 million acres that the new states wanted to fill with industrious people and then collect taxes and eliminate squatters. With all this land, why were people afraid of being overrun with European Catholics?

Public opinion in this region was anti-foreign. In the 1830s and 1840s, Detroit saw a huge increase in population coming from western New York and New England. They preferred New England ideals and values, such as temperance, observing the Puritan sabbath and the use of the Protestant Bible in teaching at public schools, to those of established French-Canadian Catholics. They were generally in accordance with Whig principles and hostile to foreign immigration to the Northwest.

This was the image of the ideal American for the Know Nothings: "Citizen Know Nothing," a Protestant, White person born in America to parents also born in America. *Library of Congress.*

In 1835, the editor of the *Detroit Journal and Courier*, a Whig newspaper, wrote, "The sentiment is daily and hourly becoming more general, that the institutions and liberties of American citizens are in danger from foreign influence....Foreigners and Catholics were the chosen instruments of the demagogues to strengthen and perpetuate their ruinous influence over the people of this country."

One factor that enflamed antagonism of the nativists of the Northwest to foreigners was a pamphlet published in London and Dublin in 1842, titled *A Proposed Plan of a General Emigration Society by a Catholic Gentleman.* The object of the pamphlet was stated in a plan to send the Irish peasants to the United States. They had to remain sober for three years and develop the land. As a reward, they would receive free passage to the Northwest and ten acres of land. The American Home Missionary Society was the main source of all evangelism in remote parts of the United States. The American Home Missionary Society published large portions of the pamphlet that were widely circulated. The pamphlet stated that the reasons for increased immigration were: 1) to dispose of surplus population, 2) to create a demand for British manufactured goods in the United States and 3) to make Roman Catholic religion dominant in America.

The American Home Missionary printed a map from the pamphlet that showed the most desirable places to settle, which included Wisconsin, Michigan, Indiana, Ohio, Illinois and a part of Iowa. The conclusion of the article was, "*Now* is the time to save the West." It added later, "The territory of this nation is an unlimited and inviting field, to which human swarms are gathering from other lands."

In the same year, 1842, the "Grand Scheme" was advertised to "expose" and arouse public sentiment of the impending danger "that there is a formal conspiracy of the crowned heads of Europe to bring our republic under Papal control....There can be no doubt that many potentates and grandees of Europe desire such a result."

The bulk of the Europeans immigrating to the Northwest were Germans. One American economic historian made the general statement that five-sixths of the Irish remained east of the Appalachians, mostly in the cities; German immigrants were farmers and pushed west beyond the mountains.

As the Whig candidates became more strident in their fear and hatred of foreigners, the Germans in the Northwest began paying attention, and the Whigs in the 1844 presidential election realized—probably too late—that the nonnative-born population in the United States was big enough to determine the outcome of an election. They helped elect Democrat James Polk, a dark horse, over the well-known Henry Clay, a Whig.

In 1852, the presidential Whig candidate, Winfield Scott, tried to win over German voters but failed to overcome years of his own nativist anti-foreign writing, which was reprinted in Democratic newspapers. Scott and the Whigs lost overwhelmingly to the Democrat, Franklin Pierce, and it was the Whigs' last presidential election. They were falling apart.

In the 1850s, Democrats, taking the opposite position, welcomed and encouraged immigration, as stated on June 2, 1854, in the *Detroit Free Press*, a Democratic organ:

> *What these countries lose we gain. Though immigration is large, we need not impede it. We apprehend no bad consequences from its extent. The difficulty is not that we have too many laborers but too few. How could our canals and railroads be built without the strong arms of Irish and German immigrants? How could our new states and territories be settled, and their wilderness made to blossom like the rose, had there been less encouragement for aliens to flock thither and become citizens?*

As the Whig political party dissolved, extreme conservative members of the Whigs adopted the nativism of a new secret nativist political party, the Order of the Star Spangled Banner, pejoratively known as the Know-Nothings. Members, when asked about their nativist organizations, were supposed to reply that they knew nothing, hence the name. As printed in the *New York Times* on June 8, 1854, a letter to the editor read:

> *As to Foreigners....Clearly, the right to govern us or to have any share or influence in our own self-government, has never been promised in any manner whatever to those who find in the United States a refuge from oppression....I beg you consider a few facts. The foreign population in the United States is about one to fifteen [6 percent], but not withstanding this disparity, four fifths of all beggary, two thirds of all pauperism, and more than three fifths of all murders, riots, rapes, burglaries, arsons, thefts, perjuries, forgeries, and other great crimes committed in this country are committed by this small percentage of the whole population....A class without virtue and ignorant and brutal, corrupting all with whom they come in contact.*
>
> *I am content to*
> *KNOW NOTHING*
> *but God, Liberty, and our Country.*

Know-Nothing muscle battled its way against Catholics and moderate Protestants in local elections across the United States. It worked, and by 1855, when a new Congress assembled in December, forty-three members were avowed Know-Nothing candidates. The Know-Nothings were reaching out to rule the nation.

The party came to Michigan and Detroit in the mid-1850s, with its now well-known political style. On August 12, 1854, the *Detroit Free Press* reported, "Riots and street fights, broken heads and black eyes have been among the minor trophies of this highly republicanized institution."

They established a series of secret lodges on the western side of the state, held a convention in Kalamazoo and began infiltrating elections in rural counties. Michigan governor Kinsley Bingham was accused of being a Know-Nothing, as were the lieutenant governor, state treasurer and more.

Their greatest strength was reached in 1855 in Detroit, when they ran a candidate for mayor, Henry Porter Baldwin, against Democrat Henry Ledyard and lost with 2,026 votes to Ledyard's 2,798 votes. But the party did elect four aldermen in four city wards.

Ledyard won despite being roughed up by "personal distraction, spurious tickets, corruption in the election boards, machinations of a secret, midnight Order, whose agents were omnipresent and ceaselessly vigilant, were but part of the machinery set in motion to crush him [Ledyard]," as reported in the *Detroit Free Press* on March 7, 1855.

With the creation of the Republican Party in 1854, many former Whigs lost their fears of Catholics and foreigners and turned to the abolition of slavery. This spelled the demise of the Know-Nothing Party, and it disappeared before the Civil War began.

4

DARK LANTERN SOCIETIES

he terms *dark lanterns* and *dark lantern societies* were commonly used in the 1850s and 1860s. They referred to political secret organizations developed by civilians to maintain political support for or against the Civil War and acted to counter perceived nefarious activities of other civilian groups, such as the Knights of the Golden Circle (pro-South) and the Union Leagues (pro-North). While the battles and military activities got attention, these dark lanterns worked in the background on such causes as ensuring Lincoln's reelection in 1864. But they induced fear in people and could be part of treasonable activities, such as support of Confederate sabotage attempts.

KNIGHTS OF THE GOLDEN CIRCLE

The Knights of the Golden Circle (KGC) was a creation of George Washington Lafayette Bickley, who was born in Virginia but moved to Cincinnati in 1851. Bickley was a scheming con artist who married a woman of wealth and burned through her money and failed everything from book publishing to land speculation. When he tried to have his wife's money transferred to his name, his brother-in-law, a Cincinnati banker, caught him in time, and his disgusted wife threw him out. Running out of prospects and connections, he had one idea left that would bring him a brief moment of fame. As portrayed by historian Frank Klement, Bickley initially envisioned a trained military drill team that would perform intricate maneuvers for audiences across the country and all over the world. He called the order the Knights of the Golden Circle, but his vision changed a lot. Bickley was inspired by William Walker, a southerner who, in 1856, raised several private armies in the South and invaded Central American countries to establish English-speaking colonies. In Nicaragua, Walker usurped the presidency and ruled from 1856 to 1857. He was executed by the government of Honduras in 1860.

Bickley's version of this was to establish a "golden circle" of lands in the Confederate States of America, Mexico, Central America, the top of South America and the Caribbean as a kingdom of slave states. To do this, he needed to raise an army of sixteen thousand men and conquer Mexico first and establish a monarchy based on slave institutions. As soon as the fighting concluded, all of Bickley's army and its secret leaders would repair to the Mexican province of Guanajuato, where the governor at the time, Manuel Doblado, supposedly had a signed treaty with Bickley and would provide another sixteen thousand soldiers for permanent subjugation of the country. The ultimate goal was to increase the power of the southern slaveholding upper class to such a degree that it could never be dislodged, by "Southernizing" (his term) all of Mexico, which meant enslaving the entire population of Mexican peons, who would be divided up as chattel property for his order's members. The Roman Catholic Church would be removed at the point of a bayonet. (Bickley had belonged to the Know-Nothings for a while.) For control, he would support a system of passports enforced on the penalty of death. The governor of Guanajuato was already preparing his province to welcome the Knights of the Golden Circle, which would depart on the October 6, 1861.

The governor devised the ritual for the Knights, along with passwords, secret hand grips, oaths and initiation dues of one, five or ten dollars, depending on the rank you aspired to. He developed an official seal and gave himself the rank of president general of the American Legion of KGC.

The *New York Times* reported that Bickley's vision "reads rather like the dream of some mad slaveholder." While he went city to city as "General Bickley," he never raised more than one hundred men, and they were very soon demanding their money back. But the *New York Times*, like other newspapers and leaders prior to the Civil War, believed this was a legitimate project in accordance with the views of most slaveholders in the South. The secret order terrified people in the North and became known across the country. A play opened in New York City in July 1861 called *The Knights of the Golden Circle*.

It wasn't long before northern Republican operatives used the KGC against Democratic opponents. A partisan editor inserted a bogus paragraph in Bickley's secret ritual: "I further promise and swear in the presence of Almighty God and members of the Golden Circle, that I will not rest or sleep until Abraham Lincoln, now president, shall be removed out of the presidential chair, and I will wade in blood up to my knees as soon as Jefferson Davis sees it proper to march with his army to take the city of Washington and the White House to do the same." This was picked up by Republican newspapers across the north and used to hammer at Democrats. KGC "castles" were suddenly suspected everywhere. The newspaper in Niles, Michigan, the *Inquirer*, printed the bogus insert and claimed to know of two castles of KGC in Niles. The *Detroit Free Press* called it "transparent humbug." The KGC was suspected of inciting a race riot in Detroit in 1863, but there was no link established.

FRANKLIN PIERCE, A KGC SPY IN MICHIGAN

Another incident of early 1860s paranoia occurred in September 1861. Former president Franklin Pierce traveled to Michigan, visiting his former interior secretary, Robert McClelland; former senator Lewis Cass; and his sister in Saginaw. Pierce was a Democrat who had been sympathetic to the South during his term from 1852 until 1856 and continued to be highly critical of Lincoln's war policies.

A Detroit bookseller, J.A. Roys, sent a letter to Lincoln's secretary of state, William H. Seward, accusing the former president of meeting with disloyal people and saying he had heard there was a plot to overthrow the government and establish Pierce as president. Later that month, the pro-administration *Detroit Tribune* printed an item calling Pierce "a prowling traitor spy," and intimating that he was a member of the Knights of the Golden Circle. No such conspiracy existed, but a Pierce supporter, Guy S. Hopkins, sent a letter to the *Tribune* purporting to be from a member of the Knights of the Golden Circle, indicating that "President P." was part of a plot against the Union. Hopkins intended for the *Tribune* to make the charges public, at which point Hopkins would admit authorship, making the *Tribune* editors seem overly partisan and gullible. Instead,

Former president Franklin Pierce visited to Michigan and was accused of being a spy for the Knights of the Golden Circle. *Library of Congress.*

the *Tribune* editors forwarded the Hopkins letter to government officials. Seward then ordered the arrest of possible "traitors" in Michigan, which included Hopkins.

Hopkins confessed authorship of the letter and admitted the hoax, but despite this, Secretary of State William Seward wrote to Pierce, demanding to know if the charges were true. Pierce denied them, and Seward hastily backtracked. Later, Republican newspapers printed the Hopkins letter in spite of his admission that it was a hoax, and Pierce decided that he needed to clear his name publicly. When Seward refused to make their correspondence public, Pierce publicized his outrage by having a Senate ally read the letters between Seward and Pierce into the congressional record, to the administration's embarrassment.

While the fevered extravagant dreams of George Bickley were gone, others used the reputation of the KGC for more mundane work, such as espionage and sabotage. As the war dragged on, they were used in border and neutral states, like Ohio and Kentucky, to stir up Southern sympathizers. They were deployed to Canada with a plan to burn down Detroit and release Confederate prisoners held on Johnson's Island in Lake Erie. They were also planning to attack a prison holding Confederate soldiers outside of Chicago. The KGC would produce eleven thousand Southern sympathizers in Chicago and attack the prison from three sides and release thirteen thousand prisoners to return to the South and resume fighting. (The South was running out of soldiers.)

This plan, like almost all Knights of the Golden Circle plots, never delivered. All they managed to do was terrify the upper Midwest with rumor and "transparent humbug." According to some, after the Civil War, the KGC went underground, and its new mission was to support a second former-Confederate, uprising against the U.S. government. This is not a mainstream historical belief but one of the myths of the Knights of the Golden Circle that perpetuates even today.

The Wide Awakes

During Lincoln's 1860 campaign before the war, the Republicans realized that Lincoln would have to win all of the northern states' votes since he couldn't even campaign in the South, let alone win a southern state. They worried that the northern Democrat Stephen Douglas could very well win in one or more northern states, which, combined with a total win in the South, would give the Democrats the presidency. They needed to ensure that Lincoln would take all of the northern states. To do this, they sent Republican New York governor, Lincoln supporter and nationally known figure William Seward, the future secretary of state in Lincoln's cabinet, on a

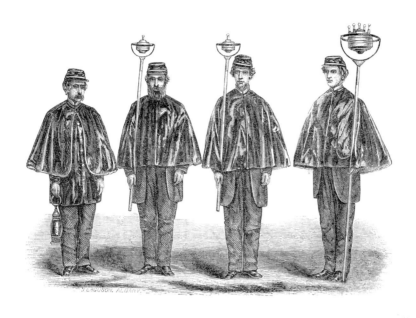

The Wide Awakes in uniform with lanterns. During the 1860 election campaign, the Wide Awakes, a marching club composed of young Republican men, appeared in cities throughout the North. *Library of Congress.*

train tour through Illinois, Indiana and Michigan. At every stop on his tour, Seward was greeted by hundreds of Wide Awakes.

The Wide Awakes were Republican Party activists and a quasi-military organization of young men, many in their teens. They marched in military style at night, wore large capes and caps of glazed black material and bore flaming kerosene lanterns carried at the end of four-foot-long poles, which could be used as weapons against rowdies if needed. The officers carried ruby or green glowing lanterns, depending on their rank. They were a sensation. Their long lines of glowing lanterns added excitement to elections and caught on across the northern states.

Seward and his family, along with Senator Ben Wade, Austin Blair and others, left New York and traveled across Canada to Detroit, where they were greeted with cannons, rockets, thousands of people and the ten companies of the Detroit Wide Awakes. Seward's speech in Detroit and the enthusiastic

Lincoln dressed in a Wide Awake uniform in a political cartoon. *Library of Congress.*

greeting he received was telegraphed across the North. Wide Awake clubs began forming all across the country. The Republicans saw how popular the Wide Awakes were and encouraged the group's growth. After the election and victory of Abraham Lincoln, the Wide Awakes staged victory parades and "jollifications." They marched once more in Manhattan, now numbering a whopping twenty-thousand marchers with lanterns and banners. They then disbanded, but their success was the start of another secret grassroots organization that would emerge in 1862—the Union League.

THE NORTH'S UNION LEAGUE

Union Clubs sprang up independently in 1860 in border states, including Missouri, Indiana, Kentucky and Tennessee, as highly secretive Union loyalists trying to nullify the work of secessionists and preventing politicians from taking their state into the Confederacy. There were even reported Union Clubs in the South, in East Tennessee, Memphis and Nashville. Kentucky had an active Union Club in Louisville. Some maintained networks of lodges controlled by a central headquarters, but they operated independently in each state.

The oath from Maryland's Union Club of 1862 was similar to other clubs and still sounds good today: "Let it be our only object to suppress the unholy rebellion which threatens the overthrow of the best and wisest government that ever existed, and hand down to our children, as our fathers did, a free, independent, prosperous and happy country."

With the publicity of the Knights of the Golden Circle growing, Unionists in states like Kentucky took strong interest in joining with other loyalists to form their own secret clubs. Union Clubs sprang up in other cities and states, like Baltimore, Maryland, and Cincinnati, Ohio.

BEGINNINGS OF A NATIONAL ORGANIZATION

In Illinois early in the war, the North was suffering a series of defeats on the battlefield, and morale in the North was waning. Unable to sell farm goods and other products to the South, many were losing their belief in the war effort. The state congress in Illinois was controlled by highly partisan Democrats, some considered pro-Southern treasonous Copperheads. The governor of Illinois was Richard Yates, who was labeled a Radical Republican, which in those days meant a Republican who was committed to the emancipation of slaves. An election was coming up in 1862, and Republicans worried about losing more control of the government to Democrats who grew bolder and more defiant every day. Men like George H. Harlow, a small-town businessman in Pekin, Illinois, conceived of an Illinois version of the secret Union Clubs made of unquestionable supporters of Lincoln and the war. They would work to bolster morale and counter the overbearing Democrats.

Harlow invited ten colleagues to start the club. Two of the invitees had been members of a Union Club in East Tennessee and provided some of the text for the oath and ritual they had participated in, along with props like an altar and candles for the lodge meetings. They called their group the Union League. They spread quickly from Chicago to Springfield. While some saw it as a counter to the KGC and war against traitors, others saw it as an extension of the Republican Party and worked with the Union League to help in saving the Union and its campaigns.

Union Clubs in Philadelphia, New York and Boston also developed. The eastern clubs were more social gatherings with opulent buildings, attracting leading men of the city to support Lincoln and the cause. Here, as elsewhere, there was real concern that Democrats would gain political might and seek peace with the South. In Boston, the Union Club held enormous public gatherings to support Lincoln's agenda.

Washington, D.C., was paying attention to the success and growth of the Union Clubs. William Osborn Stoddard was Lincoln's private secretary and, after the war, wrote about the interest Lincoln had in this movement and the need for central control in Washington for effective operations; however, Lincoln did not want the connection to Washington known. It had to appear as a grassroots movement and not part of the Republican machinery. Lincoln had been impressed by local origins and enthusiasm generated by the Wide Awakes during his first election and was concerned about the Republicans worsening political prospects, especially his own reelection coming in 1864. He was seeing many reports that told of the Republican party's disorganization and the anticipated disastrous defeat in 1864.

Lincoln began meeting with a Michigan man who was the right-hand man for Senator Zachary Chandler, Judge J.M. Edmunds. Edmunds was born in New York but moved to Ypsilanti, Michigan. In 1850, he moved to Detroit. He was involved in politics all of his adult life and ran as a Whig in the Michigan governor race but lost; however, he was highly regarded. As Stoddard described him, he was a "tall, stooping, sagacious faced, humorous looking, tobacco chewing, carelessly dressed, elderly man" but also "one of the best informed and capable politicians in the country." In 1863, he was commissioner of the General Land Office and a close personal friend of Lincoln's. Stoddard wondered why the president was in an accountable number of shut-door meetings in the executive office with a land office commissioner, but together, they secretly laid out the organization for the Union League of America, although Lincoln's hand in this was never very clear.

Edmunds held a meeting with other Lincoln friends and Republican operatives at the Interior Building. Lincoln kept his distance. Edmunds explained the Union League of America, declared himself president and chose a grand council of twelve who would direct it from Washington, and they all got started making it happen. As Stoddard wrote, "We went to work on a plan that was all ready for operation."

They opened ten councils (lodges) in Washington with success, and soon, Stoddard wrote that the Union Leagues "spread with feverish rapidity all over the north" in the winter of 1863 "under the very heat and pressure of the fall election." All the separate Union Clubs, including those in New York and other big cities, were now part of a centrally operated secret Republican election machine.

Michigan formed its Union League Council in 1863, and Zachary Chandler remained active in the council. It was clearly guided by Washington and spent its time in election activities. They did not select candidates but provided literature in the form of pamphlets to newspapers and individuals.

The Michigan League grew rapidly until halted by order of General Orlando Bolivar Willcox, a well-known figure from Detroit, in July 1863. During the war, secret societies were prohibited.

According to the *Detroit Free Press* on August 21, 1863, "A gentleman from Kalamazoo arrived in this city [Monroe, Michigan] to organize what its supporters call a secret Union League....So, it seems that General Willcox's order against such conspirators is not to be regarded."

Edmunds told the Michigan men that the Union League was no longer secret—the only secret was the central control from Washington. Consequently, he told them to "continue as if the Order had not been issued." Willcox was apparently given the word to lay off the Michigan league.

By the Spring of 1864, there were 360 subordinate councils in Michigan. The 1864 elections came, and the Republicans couldn't be happier. Lincoln returned to the White House for another term, and the Republican majority in Congress increased and gave the Republican Party control over every state legislature and governorship in the North. Edmunds gloated, "It was this organization above all others that brought about the glorious result."

After the war, the Union League continued on in Detroit as a supporter of Republican politics and a men's social club. (They seemed to play a lot of checkers and held checkers tournaments frequently.) By 1923, the Detroit Union League Club had grown to 1,200 members, and they funded and built a ten-story building on 35 Grand River in Capitol Park. (It is now called the Clark Lofts.) The Detroit Union League occupied five top floors and included a grill room, lounge, dining hall, assembly hall for balls and parties and billiard room with eight tables.

5

THE CONFEDERATE SPY RING SENT TO DESTROY DETROIT

By 1864, it was becoming clear to the South that it had lost too many men, especially Confederate officers, many of whom lingered in Northern POW camps. There was also a belief that in the North were hundreds of thousands of people who hated Lincoln—farmers who depended on Southerners to purchase goods from them—and the Midwest, or Northwest as they called it, had more of a connection to the South than to the abolitionist merchants of New England and the eastern United States. So, there was active talk and plans to demoralize Northerners and create the Northwest Confederacy by using freed Confederate prisoners and Southern sympathizers in the Northern states to burn and terrorize Northern cities along the Great Lakes, including Detroit.

From the Civil War's start, Britain sided with the South, and many believed it would enter the war on the side of the Confederacy. At the start of the war, Britain dispatched troops to Canada. Detroiters worried that if Britain entered the war as a diversion in the northern Midwest, Detroit would be a likely point of invasion. British-ruled Canada harbored Confederate leaders and spies in Toronto and even Windsor, Ontario. The mastermind of the Confederates in Canada was Jacob Thompson, whose title was special commissioner of the Confederate States in Canada and who set up headquarters in the Castle Hotel in Windsor. His first plan was to attack Chicago using seventy-five former Confederate soldiers and hundreds of Confederate sympathizers. The Democratic National Convention was being held in Chicago in August 1864. As Chicago burned, he would then send men to a Northern POW camp—Camp Douglas near Chicago—and release five thousand Confederate prisoners. This coup didn't work out, as the Confederate sympathizers failed to rally their support.

Thompson changed plans to use a small band of men to capture the only U.S. armed vessel on the Great Lakes, the gunboat USS *Michigan*. With the gunboat, he would free three thousand Confederate prisoners being held on Johnson's Island near what is now Cedar Point in Sandusky, Ohio. The freed prisoners would escape to Canada and be transferred by boat to the Bahamas and then back to the Southern Confederacy. Then, using the gunboat, he would disrupt commerce on the Great Lakes and, with a small army, pillage cities along the Great Lakes.

Thompson selected thirty-one-year-old John Yates Beall to command the enterprise. Beall was a daring, colorful Virginia aristocrat, a graduate of the University of Virginia and a member of the Virginia House of Delegates. He was a captain in Company G, Virginia Second Regiment, serving in the original Stonewall Brigade. Early on in the war, he was severely wounded and unable to fight in regular service, so he joined the secret service and eventually came to Jacob Thompson in Toronto.

Thompson sent Beall to stay in the Castle Hotel in Windsor for weeks. Here he assembled a small cast of characters to wreak havoc on Detroit and other northern cities bordering Canada. It was said that he walked the streets of Detroit laying out a plan to embarrass the United States government and demoralize the Northern spirit for the war. He and a group of twenty-five men were planning to burn half of the city. They were to start by starting a fire north of the city on the Gratiot Road, which would draw away the fire department steamer engines. At that time, his group would move to the two railroad stations in the city and start large fires at each station. Three men would pose as travelers and check in at three of Detroit's largest hotels. They would start fires in their rooms, lock the doors and slip away long before the alarm would be set off. In addition, he planned to burn steamships of the Cleveland line docked at Detroit and rent a store in the center of town, store barrels of dynamite in the store and set them off. The operation suffered, as did most of Jacob Thompson's activities, due to men betraying the plot. When one of the three hotel incendiaries failed to show up in Detroit on Jefferson Avenue, the planned meeting spot of the saboteurs, Beall rightly figured he'd deserted the team and divulged their plan, so Beall called off the operation.

But Thompson was not done. He ordered Beall and his gang to hijack a local passenger steamer to help take over the USS gunboat *Michigan*. Another man, Charles H. Cole, a former Confederate officer, would ingratiate himself with the officers of the *Michigan* and, at the right time, would drug their drinks during dinner. When the officers were unconscious, Cole would signal to Beall that he had control of the *Michigan*. Beall and his crew would then take over the *Michigan* and go on to free the Confederate prisoners on Johnson's Island. They didn't lack for ambition; you could almost hear the late-night villainous laugh from Thompson from the Windsor Castle Hotel.

Beall decided on Monday, September 19, that he would take over a steamer that regularly carried people and freight back and forth from Detroit to Sandusky, with stops on the western islands in Lake Erie. The steamer was named the *Philo Parsons*. But like the scheme to burn Detroit, counterespionage officers in Detroit learned of the plan and sent a warning to the captain of the USS *Michigan*. The captain had Charles Cole arrested and moved the *Michigan* to the edge of Sandusky Bay, where he could control his position on the lake and keep within gun shot of Johnson's Island.

Beall and his crew boarded the *Philo Parsons* in Detroit and in Sandwich, a small town next to Windsor. The plan was to take over the steamer once they reached the open water of Lake Erie. They stopped in Amherstburg, down from Sandwich, where more Confederates boarded. Twelve miles into the lake, the passengers from Detroit, Sandwich and Amherstburg turned into Confederate soldiers. Beall held a pistol to the man at the ships wheel, saying, "I am a Confederate officer. There are thirty of us, well-armed. I seize this boat and take you as prisoners." Beall ordered the pilot to stay on course while the other Confederates locked some crew members in cabins and others were sent below to the ship's hold. It was about 5:00 p.m. They were too early; the planned rendezvous with the USS *Michigan* was to be in the night, so Beall ordered the ship to turn back and dock at Middle Bass Island. At Middle Bass, they took on wood for fuel and released the steamer's crew, except the pilot, engineer and fireman needed to sail the boat. They released the remaining innocent passengers. They robbed the clerk of all ship's funds. Finally, they dumped a load of pig iron and other freight to improve the vessel's speed. At Middle Bass was docked another passenger ship, the *Island Queen*. They took control of that boat as well, tying it to the *Philo Parsons* to tow it. Soon after heading back to Sandusky, they scuttled it on a reef.

They left Middle Bass at a full head of steam to Sandusky, which they reached hours before midnight. It was a clear, moonlit night. Beall in the pilot house could see Johnson's Island and the gunboat USS *Michigan*. But it was oddly dark. He waited for the arranged signal from the main mast that the Confederates had control of the gunboat, but none came. Beall realized something had gone wrong.

The Confederate gang grew uncertain and gathered in the main cabin. Together they ordered Beall to abandon the venture and return to Windsor. He had no choice but to comply.

They arrived back at the Detroit River at 4:00 a.m. Beall, out of bombast, unfurled the Confederate flag and flew it from the flagpole on the *Philo Parsons*. The pilot, engineer and fireman, the only remaining steamer crew, were put ashore on Fighting Island.

When they docked at Sandwich at 8:00 a.m. on September 20, they opened a feed pipe and the ship began to take on water. Like true pirates, the Confederates began stealing valuables and wrecking furniture and fixtures as the boat settled into the water. They then jumped over the side. Most were apprehended by Canadian customs officers.

Beall escaped and, with Jacob Thompson, moved operations to the Niagara frontier. On December 16, Beall, with help of two Confederate officers and two others, put obstructions on a train track that ran from Dunkirk, New York, to Buffalo at a suspension bridge over the Niagara River to derail the train and kill passengers. He was arrested while returning to Canada by John S. Young, chief of the Metropolitan Detective Police; positively identified by a witness in a police lineup; and taken to Governor's Island in New York, where in 1865, he was charged for the attempted train sabotage, the *Philo Parsons* escapade and his espionage and guerrilla acts in Detroit during 1864. (The newspapers referred to Beall as the pirate of Lake Erie.) While some, including Jefferson Davis, made the claim that he was a soldier doing his duty and should be treated as a prisoner of war, he was convicted as a spy committing and breaking the "laws of war"; he was never in uniform when doing the acts and intended to injure and kill unarmed civilians. In the time of the Civil War, the penalty for these charges was death, and Beall was ordered to be hanged on February 18.

Beall was visited by his parents, two friends and an Episcopal minister. He voiced no remorse. The gallows for Beall did not have a drop floor but were considered more modern, with a series of weights and pulleys hidden behind a partition, which jerked the condemned man into the air, breaking his neck and killing him quickly. This was less offensive to the audience. Mounting the steps of the gallows, Beall was given a chair to sit on while the minister read from the Book of Prayer. He turned in his chair to face south during the reading. The reading ended, the chair was removed, the noose was put around Beall's neck and a black hood covered his head. Standing behind

Beall, the provost marshal gave a flourish with his sword, and Beall jerked off the ground. He hung for twenty minutes, when the post surgeon declared him "extinct."

It was reported by the *New York Times* that John Beall's was the first execution in New York since the hanging of Major John André, a British army officer who negotiated with the American general Benedict Arnold and was executed as a spy by George Washington during the American Revolution.

6

AFRICAN AMERICAN MYSTERIES

THE ORDER OF THE MEN OF OPPRESSION

The image for many Americans of the Underground Railroad is escaped Black slaves being secretly guided from the South to the North in the dead of night from farm to farm by courageous White abolitionists, usually Quakers or Methodists. Probably the most famous example was that of John Brown, who moved throughout the South gathering slaves and hiding them in wagons under extreme danger. Levi Coffin, a Quaker from Cincinnati, is called the unofficial president of the Underground Railroad. An example in Michigan was Dr. Nathan Thomas in the tiny town of Schoolcraft, which is near Kalamazoo. Dr. Thomas, an ardent Quaker abolitionist, was asked to open his home as a station. During the twenty years the station was in operation, Thomas and his wife aided 1,000 to 1,500 escaping slaves by providing food, shelter, medical aid and encouragement. They were typically well-educated, middle-class or wealthy White social reformers hiding Black people in attics, basements or barns.

But that's by far not the entire picture. From colonial times to the Civil War, Black slaves escaping from the South often settled in communities in the free North. Ypsilanti, by 1850, had one hundred Black people living on the south side of the city. Ypsilanti historian Matt Siegfried, who has been researching this community for several years, has concluded that many, if not most, Black residents in Ypsilanti were born in Kentucky, Missouri or Canada and had been passengers on the Underground Railroad. The Canadian born had fugitive slave parents who made it to freedom in Canada

Poster for the Detroit Underground Railroad, 1856. *Silas Farmer, Public domain.*

but returned to live in Michigan. There was regular travel from Ypsilanti to Canadian settlements like Buxton or Amherstburg, Ontario, for family gatherings and homecomings until well after World War II. Ypsilanti was not alone in this. Siegfried identified other towns in the North with Black settlements, including Lambert Lands or Mount Pleasant in Ohio and Weaver and Lost Creek in Indiana. Such places were crucially important in hiding and protecting fugitive slaves from slave hunters, especially in the 1850s, after the Fugitive Slave Act passed, and slave owners could send armed agents to retrieve escaped slaves in northern "free" states. Specific people, such as Asher Aray, known as "Brother Ray," and George McCoy, smuggled fugitives from Ypsilanti to Detroit or other cities on the Detroit River, like the city of Wyandotte.

Detroit was the busiest Underground Railroad station in pre–Civil War America due to its proximity to Canada. It is estimated that as many as forty thousand Black men, women and children passed through Detroit on the Underground Railroad to reach Canada. Like Ypsilanti, Detroit became a home for free Black people but also fugitive slaves.

William Lambert. *Public domain.*

To help get people to Canada, several organizations operated in the city, such as the Detroit Anti-Slavery Society. The society not only demanded the abolition of slavery but also focused attention on "the elevation of our colored brethren to their proper rank as men." This was short-lived and was followed by the Colored Vigilant Committee of Detroit. It was formed on December 20, 1842, by prominent Black residents of Detroit, including William Lambert. This organization helped more than 1,500 fugitives escaping to Canada during the 1850s.

With the dangers of the Fugitive Slave Act of 1850, the clandestine society called the African American Mysteries, also known as the Order of the Men of Oppression, was begun by the remarkable William Lambert. While shrouded in a great deal of mystery, the organization's purpose was to help escaped slaves and get them to free territory.

William Lambert was born free in Trenton, New Jersey, in 1817. Lambert was taken under the wing of a Quaker schoolmaster, Abner Hunt Francis, who educated Lambert and introduced him to the abolitionist movement at a young age. They moved to Buffalo, New York, and in the 1830s, Lambert traveled the Great Lakes as a cabin boy on commercial steamers. In this way, he visited Detroit. In his early twenties, he stayed in Detroit and involved himself in business and the Black community. To support himself, he worked for a tailor and eventually became a very successful businessman, leaving a significant fortune when he passed away in 1890. The Second Baptist Church was Detroit's oldest Black church, and Lambert was a founding member. In 1846, Lambert left Second Baptist Church and played a key role in establishing St. Matthew's Protestant Episcopal Mission. As he had done at the previous church, he was a leader in biblical and general education, particularly teaching Sunday school.

Lambert's secret order began by using large dray wagons with false bottoms, where they could hide three adults. Lambert described how they went into the South and, through a very secret chain of conductors and via off-road byways, would get fugitives to Detroit and eventually Canada.

Men were admitted to the order to be conductors or other roles through an elaborate ritual. As Lambert described for the *Detroit Tribune* on January 17, 1887, "[The conscript] was clad in rough and ragged garments, his head was bowed. His eyes blindfolded and an iron chain put about his neck. When his examination was over his eyes were unbound and he was admitted to the fellowship of the degree of captive. When he passed to that of the redeemed the chain and fetters were stricken off, although before that, when his eyes were unbound and he was a captive, he found about him all the members of the lodge present, each of them with a whip in his hand. In this way the organization maintained its typical character."

The organization used passwords, secret signs and elaborate rituals for new members. Lambert was a Mason and Odd Fellow in high standing, and similar to the fraternal clubs, he devised five degrees, that of rulers, judges and princes, chevaliers of Ethiopia, sterling black knights and knights of St. Domingo. The grand lodge of the society was on Jefferson Avenue between Bates and Randolph Streets.

He continued in the *Detroit Tribune*:

> *When we had received the people at the lodge we then took them to the rendezvous, which was the house of J.C. Reynolds, an employee of the company then constructing the Michigan Central railway. He had been sent by Levi Coffin of Cincinnati, who was the head of the underground railway in the west. His residence was at the foot of Eighth street, just opposite the place where the first elevator was subsequently built. The house has long since been torn down. We would fetch the fugitives there, shipping them into the house by dark one by one. There they found food and warmth, and when, as frequently happened, they were ragged and thinly clad, we gave them clothing. Our boats were concealed under the docks, and before daylight we would have everyone over. We never lost a man by capture at this point, so careful were we, and we took over as high as 1,600 in one year.*

Lambert chose to keep his secret organization primarily Black. Slave catchers were White, and before the Civil War, some of the abolitionist organizations in the city, while devoted to ending slavery, would not admit Black people to their memberships. It might have added to Lambert's caution when working with White people. In an interview many years later, Lambert said, "We began the organization of a more thorough system and we arranged passwords and grips, and a ritual, but we were always suspicious of the white man, and so those we admitted we put to severe tests, and we had one ritual for them alone and a chapter to test them in. To the privileges of the rest of the order they were not admitted."

Lambert claimed to have close connection with John Brown, and when John Brown, his men and eleven fugitive slaves came to Detroit on March 12, 1859, he was greeted by Lambert. On May 8, at 10:00 a.m., Brown held a "convention" in Chatham, Ontario that included twelve White people and thirty-four Black people.

They began with preliminary issues at a small log cabin on Prince Street, and then the group moved to the First Baptist Church on King Street. Disguising the true purpose of the convention, they claimed the meeting was to inaugurate a Masonic lodge for Black men in Chatham. The true purpose of the secret meeting was to go over Brown's plans to establish a revolutionary government of freed slaves based in the Appalachian Mountains. At the First Baptist Church, the declaration of independence and the constitution of the new republic was approved. William Lambert attended. The direct result of this meeting was the famous attack on Harpers Ferry in October 1859.

In a book by John Hinton, published in 1894, called *John Brown and His Men*, the author, who was also a friend of John Brown's, cited diary notes written in 1858 by one of John Brown's men, George B. Gill, who attended the Chatham convention. Gill wrote about Lambert and a "Secret Negro Order" he called the "League of Freedom." Gill described his conversation in Milan with another attendee of the Chatham convention named Reynolds. He stated that the African American Mysteries was a well-armed militant group that operated in states throughout the South. They intended to be part of John Brown's insurrection against the South to free slaves.

A newspaper interview with an associate of Lambert's, George DeBaptiste, also claimed in 1870 that John Brown and Lambert's secret order used a code to communicate with each other via telegraph. However, other than the details given by Lambert decades after the club ceased to be, little is known about its operations outside of Michigan.

Lambert worked closely with George DeBaptiste, a Detroiter. DeBaptiste was also a freedman and came to Detroit in 1849 in his early thirties. He already had had a varied career that included being the personal valet of President William Henry Harrison in the White House. In Detroit, he started as a barber, moved to a men's tailor shop and then bought a bakery, but with business skills, he managed to amass a fortune in everything from running a commercial steamship moving goods (and fugitive slaves) from the United States to Canada. He was also a successful caterer, according to the *Detroit Free Press*, on February 23, 1868, "In the house of Mrs. John Hull where a fine and bountiful repast was set up under the catering skills of George DeBaptiste consisting of excellent Mocha coffee, oysters, turkey, etc."

DeBaptiste was not only an astute businessman, but he was also a courageous and tireless supporter of Black causes before and after the Civil War and worked in close association with William Lambert. His experience with the Underground Railroad began before he came to Detroit, and in Detroit, along the river, he maintained several small boats hidden under docks, which he would use nightly to get fugitives over to Canada.

In his obituary on July 25, 1876, the *Detroit Daily Post* wrote, "Mr. De Baptiste led a rather eventful life, saw much of men and things, and always showed himself a bold, uncompromising advocate of right and justice, a firm friend of the poor and oppressed, and in every station an honorable, high minded gentleman."

PART II.

VICTORIAN DETROIT

7

BRASS KNUCKLE POLITICS ALONG THE DETROIT RIVER

In the nineteenth century, the most feared neighborhood in Detroit was along the river, called the Potomac Quarter. The Potomac Quarter ran east of Brush Street to Beaubien along Atwater, Franklin and Woodbridge Streets. Detroit's riverfront had wharves, like most seaports, and hosted sailors, tug men, longshoremen and other laborers, or mechanics, who lived the off season (winter) in sailor lodging houses and whore houses ("snug harbors") and spent hours in the innumerable low-lit saloons of the area. Many policemen were justifiably afraid to work in the Potomac, as the newspapers reported frequent and vicious assaults on police when they tried to make arrests.

According to the *Detroit Free Press* on August 12, 1880, "Shortly before four o'clock yesterday after noon, patrolman Theo Newton was notified of a case wherein a farmer had been robbed and upon visiting the unfortunate person had Rowena and Eva Mackey—both notorious, pointed out as the alleged robbers.…Officer Newton arrested the Mackey girls and started out with them to the Police Central Station. On the way he was assaulted by a mob of roughs, and although Newton fought pluckily his prisoners were rescued."

Men like Jem Cummerford, William Burns, Duke Morrison, Tom Manion and Jim Whitson fought with other gangs in the Potomac with revolvers, but they also threw Bowie knives at enemies across saloons and, in vicious close-up fights, gouged out eyes, bit off ears and noses, battered heads, crushed faces with brass knuckles and stomped men with hobnailed boots. This was evidenced in a report in the *Detroit Free Press* on January 29, 1878:

"Officer McPherson heard a great commotion in Jem Cummerford's saloon on Woodbridge Street, and entering he found Cummerford holding Robert Quinn to the floor and at the same time vigorously chewing one of his ears."

The common crime was to spot farmers or travelers ("greenies") with pockets of money, buy them drinks at the local holes, drug their drink and then rob them of everything, including shoes and clothing, and dump them unconscious behind the saloon.

During election times, these gangs were paid for what amounted to waging war against political opponents. The biggest user of the Potomac Gang and others, such as the McGuire brothers, was Detroit mayor William G. Thompson.

William G. Thompson and the Potomac Gang

Detroit had two mayors named William Thompson. William B. Thompson served from 1907 until 1908 and again from 1911 until 1912. William G. Thompson served as mayor from 1880 until 1883. While William B. Thompson got through his two terms without major incident, William G. Thompson seemed to be at the center of every disreputable political misdeed of the late nineteenth century.

Thompson was born in New York, served in the Civil War and ended up coming to Detroit in the early 1870s. He married Adelaide Brush, a daughter of the Elijah Brush dynasty, who died young, and Thompson was wealthy from then on as manager of the Brush estate (former Brush farm that ran up the eastern side of Woodward Avenue). He was described as scholarly and witty and fastidious in his appearance; Thompson got his hair cut daily. But he was notorious for his immoral behavior. In short, Thompson was a cad. In 1888, Thompson was party to a sensational and public fight in which he was considerably pummeled by his brother-in-law Daniel Campau. Campau warned Thompson that "he must not talk about his wife hereafter in barrooms and other public places, as he had been doing," This event that made national news. He was infamous for his sexual appetite, regarded as a serious character fault among the wealthy Detroiters in the Victorian Age. Thompson's favorite and most-talked-about mistress was a Black woman who was the sister of his barber, Dapper Dan. Thompson liked to dress her in the finest fashions of the day, which appalled Detroit's high society. He was also suspected of having mistresses younger than sixteen years old.

Thompson first ran for office, chief magistrate of the city, as a Republican in 1875. The *Detroit Post*, then the Republican news organ, wrote about Thompson: "His native instincts coupled with his egotistical ambition, have let him into affiliation with the worst elements of the population who have been artfully leagued together in almost all the wards to secure his nomination."

That was William G. Thompson's political modus operandi for the next two decades. He hired "roughs and bummers" from the Potomac Quarter to crash conventions; shout down speakers; steal ballot boxes; severely beat up political enemies; work the wards as repeat voters, or "repeaters" as they were called then; and generally create mayhem to steal nominations. His main support was in the Seventh Ward, which ran from Jefferson up Russell Street, along what is today the Eastern Market.

In 1880, the year he first ran for mayor, the newspapers reported, "Thompson contributed much to the disgraceful character of the howling proceedings" by way of "getting their hand in" a gang of perhaps as many as 125 rough and readys first invaded the Tenth Ward caucus which they tried to override and brow beat."

The gang then moved onto the Seven Ward Caucus, which was held at a beer saloon. They were joined by others from the Potomac Gang, brought in by the wagonload to stuff the ballot box. Republicans of long-standing were said to have been denied the opportunity to vote. A witness claimed that Thompson, never one for subtilty, held the ballot box in his arms and covered the slot.

Thompson's most outrageous acts occurred in his run for mayor in 1891. The Republicans denied Thompson the nomination for mayor, so Thompson decided that he would run as a Democrat to campaign against the Democratic nominee Judge John Miner. Hazen Pingree was the current mayor, and he was fighting hard against the City Railway Company to lower streetcar fares. The street railway consequently backed Thompson with thousands of dollars. After weeks of campaigning in the saloons and slums to buy the votes of caucus delegates, Thompson was failing, so he changed tactics: he would storm the Democratic Convention by brute force with an armed mob of Potomac Gang members.

The convention was being held at Harmonie Hall, and convention chairman William Shield had learned that the Thompson men would attack the hall, so he had the doors locked and barricaded.

On October 20, 1891, Thompson and the gangs arrived and began battering the doors down while another group entered an adjacent building,

Harmonie Hall in Detroit, 1870s.
Silas Farmer, public domain.

went to the third floor and, with a wooden ladder, smashed a Harmonie Hall window, laid the ladder between the buildings and crawled across to the hall. Once inside the hall, they quickly unlocked the side doors, and the "armed thugs and desperados" poured into the convention shouting for William G. Thompson's nomination and beating up legitimate delegates. The streetcar company made arrangements with the chief of police to hold back police from chasing out the gang members from the hall, and things looked bleak. Chairman William Shield, realizing what was happening, gathered leaders into a separate meeting room, and they quietly nominated John Minor as the Democratic nominee. Thompson was defeated.

Of course, Thompson wasn't finished causing mayhem. In 1892, he was part of an affray in which the city's most notorious gangster, Johnny Considine, was shot in the chest in Tom Swan's saloon in downtown Detroit. Thompson was drinking with others when he slipped an open box of black shoe polish in the pocket of one of his companions' new suit. The victim, Tom McCarty, accused Thompson of the deed, and in response, Thompson slapped his face. McCarty punched him, so Considine grabbed McCarty, and he and two others punched and kicked McCarty on the floor. McCarty managed to get up and was covered in blood. McCarty was armed and pulled out his pistol and shot Considine at point-blank range, and then he and Thompson slipped out a side door. Considine was carried out but died, and since he was part of a family gang that had a rule of never reporting anything to the police, the gang took care of justice.

William G. Thompson walked away unscathed.

8

THE DISCIPLES OF
THE FLYING ROLL

The twelve lost tribes are to gather at Detroit, that the scripture may be fulfilled.
—Flaming Sword, *February 9, 1892*

Michael Xavier Mills was born in Elgin County, Ontario, in 1856 and, for thirty years, led an uneventful, if not unremarkable, life. At age twenty-one, he married a local woman, Rosetta Close, and they had two children—one died at age five. They moved to Sarnia, Ontario, and from there to Port Huron and Lexington. Then they decided to move to Detroit, where Mills became acquainted with the writings of James Jezreel, which would utterly change their lives.

Jezreel, an Englishman, was born James White, a soldier in the British Sixteenth Regiment, and he declared himself the Sixth Messenger of the Christian Israelite faith. This was a sect that was one of several variations begun in the eighteenth century by Joanna Southcott in Devon, England. Southcott was a domestic servant, who, in her later years, was reported to have visions. She claimed to have up to ten thousand followers. After her death, the sect splintered, and one branch James Jezreel followed. In short, the sect believed that Christians were in error living by only the gospels and ignoring the laws of the Old Testament. One had to do both. They were Nazarites so refused to cut their hair or beards, never drank alcohol or smoked and ate only kosher food. They did not believe in marriage. They believed that at death the body perishes but the soul remains, but instead of rising to heaven, it enters another living person, until all people on earth

Members of the Israelite House of David from Benton Harbor, Michigan, who called on the president to extend their thanks for action taken while they were in camp as drafted men. The members of the House of David believe that the hair and beard should be allowed to grow naturally, and the president issued an executive order that their religious belief be undisturbed when they were drafted into the army. *Photo made at the White House; Library of Congress.*

will be members of the sect. They followed the Flying Roll, which was not some kind of sushi or a food fight. James Jezreel wrote a book in 1879 called, *The Extracts of the Flying Roll*, based on the vision of the Prophet Zachariah: "Then I turned, and lifted up mine eyes, and looked, and behold a flying roll. And he said unto me, What seest thou? And I answered, I see a flying roll; the length thereof is twenty cubits, and the breadth thereof ten cubits."

The roll (think scroll) listed 144,000 people, 12,000 from each of the twelve tribes of Israel who would be spared by God from a horrible death at the end of the world. In 1880, Jezreel came to America to do missionary work, and he developed converts in several cities across the United States, including Detroit, Grand Rapids and Benton Harbor.

After arriving in Detroit and reading Jezeel's book, Mills began selling the books door to door. After three years, Mills had the revelation that he was the seventh (and final) messenger, and he now called himself Prince Michael (as described in the Old Testament book of Daniel), who was chosen by

God to gather the 144,000 and lead them to the New Israel and salvation. They were officially called the Disciples of the Flying Roll, and Detroit was, as Mills called it, the "city of deliverance." It was known as the great Ingathering of Israel.

Mills claimed to have already been freed of the uncleanness of Adam. He wrote, "I thought I was being torn to pieces. I was thrown to the ground and balls of fire flew from all parts of my body. I suppose I said 'Praise God' ten thousand times. I am freed from all bodily infirmity and all food, that which before was agreeable, disagrees with me."

Hundreds of Flying Rollers came from Canada and cities in the United States, such as Richmond, Indiana, to escape the wrath of God and the end of the world and to stay at the God House at 47 Hamlin Street (currently Bethune Street) in Detroit.

On February 10, 1892, the *Detroit Free Press* reported, "The Richmond families who have forsaken old friends, homes and kindred for the new prophet are B.F. Purnell and his wife and children and Mr. and Mrs. Lewis Dawson and their little ones. George Primrock and his family, William Knott, Marion Wallace and his family are the other converts."

They sold their belongings, including their homes and farms, and brought considerable money with them, which Mills used to buy additional houses in what was then far north Detroit to house his flocks.

In the beginning, the newspapers were friendly toward the odd group. "They are despite contumely and ridicule a brave, open hearted class of people," reported the *Detroit Free Press* on February 10, 1892.

But things changed quickly for the disciples. In March 1892, Michael's wife, Rosetta Close, filed for divorce, which was covered daily in the newspapers. She claimed that he subjected her to humiliation and torture and slept with other women in the sect who lived in the house on Hamlin Street. In addition, some of the female members brought their children with them and left their husbands behind. One husband sued for custody, which was likewise covered in the newspapers. Neighbors near the sect were beginning to complain of the notoriety their street was getting since the Flying Roll began buying up houses. They complained to police that sect members were "lazy, thriftless, sensual people." Members became afraid to leave the houses, as rowdies and college boys gathered on their street at night to heckle them and throw stones and buckets of tar at their houses.

According to the *Detroit Free Press* on March 5, 1892, "Every car brought more and at 8 o'clock, Hamlin Avenue, from Woodward Avenue to the Israelites' houses were a solid mass of people. There must have been 1,000 boys and young men all hooting and making all sorts of threats against Prince Michael and his followers. Many were armed with stones and brickbats and had it not been for the timely arrival of a squad of police would have done serious injury to the houses." Police started to block off the street to prevent violence.

Finally, Mills was accused of seducing a young fifteen-year-old girl, Bernice Bickle. Bernice was the daughter of two sect members and was invited to the sect by Michael to play the piano during religious services. Mills, with help from his assistant, Eliza Court, repeatedly kept the girl up late at night for Bible studies. Eliza Court and Mills pressured the girl to stop resisting the will of God. Eventually, she did.

In a trial that took place in the summer of 1892 in Ann Arbor, since it was decided that a fair trial was not possible in Detroit, the details of the seduction came out. Michael was attracted to the teenager, and even Bernice's parents encouraged her to sleep with Mills, as he was a prophet, and therefore, it was ordained by God. As her father stated in the trial, "Michael was to be her husband and to have charge of Bernice." He declared from the witness chair to the packed courtroom: "Michael is Christ, her husband."

Mills was found guilty and sent to state prison in Jackson, Michigan. Eliza Court continued to run the Flying Roll sect until Mills was released. In 1897, Eliza Court tried to resettle the Flying Roll across the river in Windsor, but the Windsor populace wanted nothing to do with them. Eventually, the sect disbanded.

Rebirth of the House of David

But it was not finished. The group reemerged at the turn of the century as the House of David and settled a colony in Benton Harbor. Somehow, while rejected in Detroit, the group thrived in Benton Harbor. The new seventh messenger was Benjamin Franklin Purnell. The press called him King David and his wife, Mary Pollard Purnell, Queen Mary, which rankled their followers, who always referred to them as Brother David and Sister Mary. They bought a mansion to live in and called it Shiloh, and they had over one thousand members coming from all parts of the world. In 1908, they bought 180 acres around the mansion and started an amusement park, which drew 100,000 tourists a year. They had a band and a baseball team that held national attention as a semipro team playing exhibition games with big league teams like the Chicago Cubs. (Benjamin Purnell was supposedly a big sports fan.) One pitcher was offered a lucrative contract to play for the White Sox, but he had to cut his shoulder-length hair and shave his beard. He refused. The House of David started the team to give the young men of the sect something to keep them from leaving.

On August 25, 1930, the *New York Times* reported, "Benton Harbor, Mich. The New York Giants defeated the House of David team in a twilight exhibition game tonight, 6-1 before a crowd of 10,000." The baseball team was funded by the House of David until 1956.

As before, they were awaiting the "ingathering," when 144,000 members listed on the flying roll would gather at the House of David. They were carried by the biblical words, "In that day the House of David shall be as God, as the Angel of the Lord before them." But also, as before with Michael Mills, Benjamin Purnell was accused of sexual relations with minors—the Bramford girls, daughters of a member. This resulted in a raid by the Michigan State Police and county sheriffs. One of the girls claimed that she was assaulted as young as ten years old, but Purnell was never convicted. Purnell's wife and other members of the sect claimed that the girls were vindictive because their father had brought a large sum of money to the sect and they believed they were entitled to some of it. Once again, there were lurid tales in the newspapers about gross sexual misconduct and shocking talk of "purification rites."

Benjamin Purnell died in 1927 amid scandal, debt and infighting between his wife, Mary, and the board of trustees. His followers set up his coffin in the Shiloh House and waited for three days for his resurrection. When nothing changed, they had him embalmed and he remained in the house thereafter.

Mary broke away from the House of David with a small band of followers and founded the City of David, or more formally the Israelite House of David as reorganized by Mary Purnell, not far away. It remained in existence until her death at age ninety.

By the mid-1960s, the members were mostly over sixty-five years old, and the amusement park and the other tourist attractions were still barely going, but the baseball team, band and other features were gone. The House of David more resembled a monastery or nunnery than a spurious end-of-the-world religious cult. The members who remained maintained a large orchard, continued to grow wheat and grains and kept up an expansive vegetable garden. They kept bees, ran a bakery and maintained a communal laundry. There was an electrical shop and a craft shop, and they made excellent House of David ice cream, which they sold in a small shop. No one feared starvation, as they kept up a vegetarian restaurant. Clothing was provided, as well as shelter and dormitory-style rooms. As one newspaper reporter described them in 1966, "Benjamin's followers today seem to dwell in a peaceful and harmonious accord that one might envy."

9

CRUSADE OF FEAR

THE AMERICAN PROTECTIVE
ASSOCIATION IN DETROIT

On March 13, 1887, a sixty-year-old lawyer named Henry F. Bowers founded the American Protective Association (better known in its day as the APA) in the town of Clinton, Iowa. The APA tried to revive long-held suspicions that Catholics could not be considered fully American because of their religious connections to Rome. It was a secret society with a rabid loathing of Catholics, especially Irish, and the founders were surprised that it grew to a national movement; by 1893, it had seventy thousand members in twenty states, including Michigan and Detroit, where the APA supreme president lived and printed the newsletter the *American Patriot*.

But why in Clinton, Iowa, or Saginaw or Detroit was there such hatred of Catholic immigrants at the end of the nineteenth century? Many of the small towns had very few Catholics, and they were dwarfed by enormous migrations of Protestants from the East. Since 1870, many anti-Catholic groups had started in rural areas and died after achieving local political goals or faded away out of disinterest. The men who founded the APA became alarmed when a local Catholic priest had apparently tried to influence the votes of his parishioners in an election, although local political and economic factors also played a role in the APA's origins. But somehow the APA spread across the country with its major interest in the midwestern states.

According to Henry Desmond, who wrote in 1912 about the APA, there were several issues fueling this fear. First, much of the hatred was the historic fear Protestants had of the Catholic Church; much of the virulent hatred was fueled by Protestant preachers. In Detroit, there were frequent combative protests about public funding for Catholic schools. Public schools had Bible studies and other religious activities based on the Protestant King James Bible and general Protestant teachings. The Catholics insisted on a Catholic focus for their children or at least a secular education for all. APA saw this as an attempt to destroy Protestantism.

Catholics were rising in social and economic status, which was causing envy in some people; Catholics were laborers, but some were going to college and becoming doctors, editors and more.

In October 1892, it was the 400th anniversary of Christopher Columbus's "discovery" of America. This was a point of deep pride for Catholics, and they held parades or demonstrations of schoolchildren or Catholic societies sometimes dressed in uniforms, causing bigotry and fear that Catholics might take over America; the APA considered Columbus a dubious part of U.S. history. In 1893, the World's Columbian Exhibition was held in Chicago. The APA declared the event to be a plot of Catholics to promulgate the pope and their religion. The APA flooded newspapers and legislatures with anti-"Romanist" documents.

The APA's tactics to combat Catholics was much like what we see today in extreme right-wing political and social groups: in-your-face combative patriotism and exaggerated, if not completely fictitious, stories and rumors repeated over and over, in this case about the pope, priests and nuns. The APA sponsored lectures by former priests and nuns, or those claiming to be such, who described the horrors of life inside church and convent walls. The APA promoted the falsehood that had been started by the Know-

APA propaganda depicting the pope as an octopus whose many arms control the White House, Congress and federal financial and publishing institutions. *Art from an 1894 book*, Errors of the Roman Catholic Church.

W.J.H. Traynor, supreme president of the American Protective Association from 1893 to 1903. *Library of Congress.*

Nothings that Catholic churches hoarded guns and ammunition in secret underground vaults at the ready to take over the United States. And the APA tactics worked; following the Civil War, the nation elected seven Republican presidents, supporters and sometimes members of the APA, to one Democratic president, Grover Cleveland.

But the APA lie that terrified Protestants in 1893 was a fictitious letter published in Detroit by APA supreme president William Traynor. Traynor was originally from Brantford, Ontario. He moved to Detroit, where he was editor of the anti-Catholic weekly the *Patriotic American* and was elected supreme grand master of the Loyal Orange Institution of the United States. Many APA's most outspoken members were from the Order of the Orange in Canada, a Protestant organization started in Scotland. Traynor was elected supreme president of the American Protective Association in 1893, and he continued to head that organization during its peak of influence in the mid-1890s. He led the organization until APA founder Henry F. Bowers was returned as the group's leader in 1903.

The fictitious letter in 1891, allegedly from Pope Leo, titled "Instructions to Catholics" included orders to exterminate Protestants in the United States on the celebration of the Feast of Saint Ignatius, July 31, 1893. This was followed by tens of thousands of leaflets that copied a bogus encyclical purportedly signed by the pope to massacre Protestants. While it might seem ridiculous to consider people terrified of an attack by eight million Catholics, a significant minority in the country with sixty-one million Protestants in 1890, it was completely believed by huge numbers of people, and they joined the APA in droves.

The power of the APA to intimidate Republican politicians and operatives began to wane in 1896 during the presidential election. The APA, including Traynor, began antagonizing McKinley, one of several Republicans running for party nomination. The APA believed McKinley was soft on Romanism and reported in a circular that year: "Among the managers and supporters, secret and public, of Major McKinley are Richard Kerens, a Romanist of Missouri, who again and again denounces the APA." The APA repudiated McKinley and declared that they "would fight him to the end."

However, things were changing, and in New York, Republican leaders were weary of aggravating thousands of Italian voters, so they turned away the APA with its demands for anti-Catholic planks added to the Republican Party platform of 1896. William McKinley was elected that year. The APA began dissolving as members dropped out by the tens of thousands. In March 1897, President-Elect William McKinley's first appointment to his new cabinet was Judge McKenna of California, a Catholic. And while there were howls of bitter protest from APA officers, not a ripple was heard from both parties in Congress or any major newspaper.

10

DETROIT'S CASTLE

At the intersection of Grand River Avenue, Adams and Cass, a few things stand out about a unique building that sits alone across from what is now DTE's Beacon Park. The most obvious is that it's styled like a sandstone castle, complete with turreted towers and narrow fortress-like windows. It is also restricted to a tiny triangular cement island lot on the northwest side of downtown, as if the streets were widened and took away its space. At four stories high, it's too tall to be a Victorian house and too small to be an office building. Since 1982, commuters had driven by its boarded-up windows, but it was rehabbed and brought back to life by two brothers, Tom and David Carleton, and their friend Sean Emery. It now has a couple of restaurants and houses their marketing agency, Mindscape, with more offices for lease. But who built such a building and why?

The site was originally on the Lewis Cass farm and was donated to the city to be a marketplace, which was known as the Cass Market for years. However, in 1896, a group called the Grand Army of the Republic (the GAR) asked the city to use the site to build a Detroit GAR headquarters for the various "posts" that dotted the city. In 1901, the building was completed, and a dedication ceremony was held, presided over by then mayor Maybury, aldermen, the city controller and hundreds of Civil War veterans and GAR members, some wearing their original faded Union uniforms to officially open the GAR Memorial Hall. The dedication for the completed hall—attended by hundreds of Detroiters—was held on January 16, 1901. "Grand Old Men Now Snugly Housed," read the headline in the *Detroit Free Press*.

BUT WHO WERE THE GAR?

After the end of the Civil War, various state and local organizations were formed in the North for veterans to network and maintain connections with each other. When the war ended, many soldiers returned to isolated family farms and realized they missed the friendship and camaraderie of their fellow soldiers. These organizations also provided good opportunities to network. This was the basis of forming the Grand Army of the Republic, founded on April 6, 1866, on the principles of "Fraternity, Charity and Loyalty," in Springfield, Illinois, by Dr. Benjamin F. Stephenson. The first GAR post was established in Decatur, Illinois. Later, as the GAR grew in membership, reaching peak membership in 1890 (410,000 members), it became the first national organization to promote Republican Party politics. The support of the GAR was considered essential for Republican candidates to win nomination. The GAR's political power grew during the latter part of the nineteenth century, and it helped elect several United States presidents, beginning with the eighteenth, Ulysses S. Grant, and ending with the twenty-fifth, William McKinley. Five Civil War veterans and members of the GAR were elected president of the United States, and all were Republicans (Ulysses S. Grant, Rutherford B. Hayes, James A. Garfield, Benjamin Harrison and William McKinley.) The GAR also promoted causes, such as pensions for Black veterans, voting rights for Black people and establishing May 30 as Memorial Day.

The national GAR organization was divided into state branches called "departments" and community-level organizations called "posts," usually named after a deceased local war hero and numbered in its state department. Detroit was home to several posts: the Farquhar Post, Fairbanks Post, John Brown Post (Black), Detroit Post and the O.M. Poe Post. The building was proposed to the city by the Fairbanks Post. Fairbanks was derogatorily referred to as the "silk stockings" post by some, since many of the members came from wealthy neighborhoods.

Bruce Butgereit from Grand Rapids has an expertise in Civil War–related issues and knows the history of the times and the history of the GAR buildings across the state of Michigan. He said, "Every member wore their local post's unique uniform that included a black Stetson hat, blue double-breasted coat, blue-black trousers, and a white belt worn outside the coat with the striking G.A.R. brass belt buckle. The Fairbanks post also wore a white ascot."

In Detroit in the 1890s, there was no bigger supporter of the GAR than Mayor Hazen Pingree. Pingree was born in Maine but as a young man worked

GAR parade in Detroit in 1891. *Bentley Historical Library, University of Michigan, George Washington Merrill Papers.*

in a shoe factory in Massachusetts. In 1862, Pingree enlisted in the Union army to serve in the Civil War with the First Massachusetts Heavy Artillery Regiment (Company F). He fought in major battles and was captured and spent time in various Confederate prisons, including Andersonville.

Pingree invited GAR members to his Victorian mansion in Brush Park when they came to Detroit for their national "encampment" in 1891. Men who had endured Andersonville Prison, as he had, were invited to stay with his family overnight.

The GAR Comes to Party in Detroit

Every year, the GAR held national conventions in different cities. They called the conventions "encampments." Veterans used these events to relive some of their war experiences; hundreds of army tents were set up where members would stay. They also had campfires throughout the cities and spent evenings talking with old colleagues and reminiscing about their lives in the war.

The GAR members came to Detroit twice for the national encampment, in 1891 and 1914. In 1891, thirty thousand members marched down Woodward. According to the *Detroit Free Press* on August 5, 1891, "It was a day never to be forgotten….Detroit waved all her banners and the Grand Army marched with all her chivalry. Miles and miles of heroes who saved the Union formed a column which took six hours to pass the reviewing stand."

In 1914, ninety thousand GAR members visited Detroit. For the first time, Detroit provided automobiles to veterans who had been left crippled, maimed or feeble in the war to ride in the parade up Woodward Avenue. In the past, they were given a special reviewing section to watch the parade and their colleagues. Tens of thousands marched. One thousand musicians in separate bands marched with them and later assembled in Grand Circus Park for a concert. A two-hundred-member fife and drum corps marched as well. And from the grandstand, three thousand local children sang patriotic songs to soldiers as they passed. Downtown, thirty-three enormous portraits of Michigan veterans who had been killed in the war were mounted on trolley car poles from Jefferson to Gratiot. On Woodward, as it ends at Jefferson, were two colonnades of white columns with portraits of Union generals, called the Court of Heroes. At night, there were moonlit river rides and fireworks at Belle Isle.

The Detroit GAR Building

The main motive here was to secure in Detroit permanent free quarters for the different old soldier organizations. While some of the veterans are well-to-do and could maintain their share of the payment of rental, the mass of them are poor.
—Detroit Free Press, *December 12, 1900*

The City of Detroit agreed to help pay for the new building. The cost was split between the Detroit GAR members (who paid $6,000) and the city (which paid the remainder of the $44,000 total cost).

It was designed by Swiss-born local architect Julius Hess, who died before it was finished. Construction was completed in 1900, a week after Hess's death. The castle motif was popular at the turn of the twentieth century and is referred to as Richardsonian Romanesque, a style with a rough stone exterior, thick walls and castle-like flourishes intended to convey a sense of security and a militaristic feeling of strength. It is a theme seen in light guard armories and in churches, such as the First Presbyterian Church on Woodward Avenue in Detroit.

Structurally, the building, like many in its day, is overbuilt. Since there was no structural analysis available to architects and engineers, the practice was to be absolutely certain that something was solid, so beams, pillars and joists were all built much stronger than was actually needed. Joists seen in ceilings exposed from water-damaged plaster are enormous, made from the original Michigan pine forests. The building's features are functional rather than opulent, without the stained glass, ornately carved banisters or polished brass details of Victorian homes. The entrance doors and arched windows rise fifteen feet, but the lobby is unimpressive compared to the breathtaking vaulted ceilings of the finest Detroit buildings. A late-added elevator also takes up a large portion of the lobby.

But the building has its special beauty. Ceilings are twenty feet high in almost every room. Walls are coved or arched near the ceiling. Sunlight pours into every room from the plate-glass windows, and when combined with the high ceilings, the building seems airy and open. There doesn't seem to be a right angle anywhere. The room shapes are determined by the castle structure, with round turret rooms and wedge-shaped rooms used for card games and reading. Big doors once had sliding "peek-a-boo" slots where members might have to be approved to enter.

Historian Butgereit said, "There are GAR buildings throughout the state. Some are tiny, like the GAR building in Sunfield, Michigan. Some have been changed into museums or other functions. The GAR in St. Joseph on the river is now a children's museum. But the Detroit hall has always been special." The GAR's purpose was to give the former soldiers a social organization and to provide charity, assistance and health care to needy veterans and their families. It also paid for funerals and burials for those without means.

But by 1910, numbers of GAR members were beginning to dwindle: "Since Fairbanks Post was mustered in May 1881 there have been about 1,350 veterans placed upon its rolls. Some have withdrawn…but a far greater percentage has joined their martyr comrades in the great beyond, until now only about 300 answer 'Here!' to roll call," reported the *Detroit Free Press* on January 9, 1910.

By 1934, the veterans were too old to maintain the building and handed it over to the City of Detroit. The city converted the space into a recreation center from 1940 to 1982, when it was closed as a cost-saving move. Theodore Penland of Oregon was the GAR's final commander. In 1956, after the death of the last member, Albert Woolson, the GAR was formally dissolved. The GAR was forgotten, and its Detroit castle passed into abandonment.

11

ANARCHY COMES TO DETROIT

The problem with socialism is that it takes up too many evenings.
—*Oscar Wilde*

By the 1880s, there were two workers' holidays, Labor Day and the international and more politically incendiary International Worker's Day or May Day, May 1. May Day demonstrations were usually dominated by European immigrants, as the unemployed used the occasion to vent their anger. European unions and Socialist groups adopted it as an occasion to display their strength. New labor organizations sprang up, and old ones expanded in a wave of militancy and activism that peaked in 1886 in the "great uprising of labor," when union membership reached a new high, huge strikes shook the nation and independent labor political parties surfaced in community after community. Many of these parades drew thousands and ended in violence.

In the early 1880s through the 1890s, anarchists and Socialists were part of the Labor Day parade in New York and other cities, including Detroit. As many unions tried to dissociate with the left-wing militant political groups, some left-wing groups would sneak into the parades as they marched. On September 3, 1888, the *Detroit Free Press* reported, "An immense blood red flag was carried through the streets of Cleveland today and behind it marched a score of anarchists....The anarchists were in the procession and declaring themselves to be carpenters they were permitted to retain the place they had quietly slipped into. At the garden they unfurled their flag and refused to acknowledge the Stars and Stripes."

Anarchism began in Europe in the mid-nineteenth century. The word comes from the ancient Greek *anarkhia*, meaning "without a ruler." The basics of anarchism are that it rejects social and governmental hierarchies as unjust and advocates their replacement with self-governed societies based on voluntary cooperation. These corporative groups are often described as stateless societies. Anarchism's central disagreement with other ideologies is that it holds the state to be undesirable, unnecessary and harmful. Another form of anarchism advocates for the total freedom of the individual, to not be confined by the laws and mores of society. Anarchist philosophy claimed to have roots in prehistoric times, and several Greek philosophers advocated for a society without hierarchy and rulers. The Golden Age of Anarchy began in the French Revolution and ended with the Spanish Civil War in 1936.

Anarchy began arriving in the United States in the middle of the nineteenth century with the deluge of immigrants, especially Germans. It soon allied itself with the labor movement, especially in the big cities with thousands of immigrants. With links to labor and unions, some anarchists began advocating violence as the only means to combat the capitalist's stranglehold of the working people of the world.

THE EVENT THAT CHANGED AMERICAN'S ATTITUDE TOWARD SOCIALISM

Albert Parsons was born in Texas and served in the Confederate army. After the war, he settled in Texas and advocated for rights of former slaves. With his wife, Lucy Parsons, he moved to Chicago in 1873 and worked on newspapers. He became interested in the rights of workers and Socialism. After embracing anarchism, Albert Parsons, turned his specific cause to the growing movement to establish the eight-hour working day. On May 1, 1886, in Chicago, Parsons, with his wife and their two children, led 80,000 people down Chicago's Michigan Avenue. Over the next few days, 340,000 laborers joined the strike. Parsons, amid the May Day Strike, found himself called to Cincinnati, where 300,000 workers had gone on strike that Saturday afternoon. On Sunday, he addressed the rally in Cincinnati about the news from the "storm center" of the strike and participated in a second huge parade led by two hundred members of the Cincinnati Rifle Union, with certainty that victory was at hand. In response, unions across the United States prepared a general strike in support of the event.

On May 3 in Chicago, a fight broke out when strikebreakers attempted to cross the picket line, and two workers died when police opened fire on the crowd. The next day, anarchists staged a rally at Chicago's Haymarket Square. A bomb was thrown by an unknown party as the protests were beginning to break up, killing an officer and wounding as many as sixty. In the ensuing panic, police opened fire on the crowd, and the crowd fired back. Seven police officers and at least four workers were killed. Eight anarchists directly and indirectly related to the organizers of the rally were arrested and charged with the murder of the deceased officer. The men became international political celebrities among the labor movement. Albert Parsons was among four of the men executed, and a fifth committed suicide prior to his own execution. The incident became known as the Haymarket Affair and inspired anarchists around the world but also terrified non-working-class people with its mobs, fiery rhetoric and bombings.

Immediately after the Chicago anarchists were arrested, eight hundred Detroit men met in Germania Hall to hear speeches by the Socialist Labor Party and condemn the executions in Chicago. Samuel Goldwater addressed the angry crowd in the hall, stating, "I have taken part in this great movement both as a Socialist and an anarchist. I have never yet possessed so much as a revolver. But I say if these men hang, 100,000 men will arise to take their places."

But in general, Detroit felt immune to the violence of Chicago's anarchistic violence and similar disruptions in London and European capitals. According to the *Detroit Free Press* on December 10, 1888, "The threatened trouble with anarchists in Chicago has caused some muttering among the handful in Detroit....One of the prime reasons why anarchistic ideas have not flourished in Detroit is because legitimate labor organizations here will have none of them....Level-headed laboring men [are] refusing to have anything to do with the extremists."

In the years that followed the Haymarket explosion, May Day became an occasion for protesting the arrests of Socialists, anarchists and unionists. Detroit's militants kept a low profile, preferring to celebrate in Arbeiter Hall or Turner Hall. The halls were bedecked in red flags and bunting, with families attending. The speeches were generally in German, since, as the *Free Press* reported, nine-tenths of the attendees were German.

DETROIT'S GENTLE ANARCHIST

The most visible anarchist in Detroit was Charles Joseph Antoine Labadie (1850–1933), always referred to as Jo Labadie, an important figure in the early Michigan labor movement of the late nineteenth century. Jo Labadie was known as the "gentle anarchist." He sported a Buffalo Bill–style goatee and wore wide-brimmed hats. He was a nationally known writer, poet, philosopher and artist. He began an organization called the Fellowship of Freedom and invited intellectuals from around the United States and beyond to a forty-acre farm he moved to from Detroit in 1913. This is now Kensington Park, where he was eventually buried. The remains of the cabin and the flowers he and his wife, Sophie, planted can still be seen at the junction of the Aspen and Wildwing Trails at Kensington Metro Park. Jo Labadie invited men and women to discuss and debate controversial issues of the day in a relaxed country atmosphere. Labadie and Sophie called the farm Bubbling Waters and opened it as a retreat for working-class citizens. They invited people to use the property free of charge as long as they took care of it and tended to its needs.

He also developed an enormous collection of anarchist and other Socialist publications along with his own writings, which he eventually donated to the University of Michigan in 1911. That collection, known today as the Joseph A. Labadie Collection, is still active and remains the largest publicly available collection of radical literature in the world.

Labadie was born on a frontier farm near Paw Paw, Michigan, to parents of French and Indian descent. He moved to Detroit in 1872. He was a longtime defendant of the Haymarket anarchists and lamented that he and the anarchist movement were misrepresented by the newspapers. In 1891, he claimed that nine-tenths of the letters he received asking for information about anarchism were from native-born Americans, not immigrants. Anarchists were misunderstood; he frequently compared anarchists to nonviolent Quakers.

Labadie supported community cooperation, as he supported community control of water utilities, streets and railroads. Although he did not support the militant anarchism of the Haymarket anarchists, he fought for the clemency of the accused because he did not believe they were the perpetrators. In 1888, Labadie organized the Michigan Federation of Labor, became its first president and forged an alliance with Samuel Gompers.

The anarchists kept Detroit in edgy concern throughout the late 1880s. According to the *Detroit Free Press* on December 23, 1888, "They will be

Jo Labadie's house in Detroit.
Library of Congress.

close watching by those in authority....This afternoon [anarchists] will hold a secret meeting to take up the question of arming its members.... They made arrangements with a Detroit dealer to supply them with rifles on demand."

ANARCHY'S DARK SIDE

Leon Czolgosz might be labeled as Jo Labadie's dark opposite. He was an anarchist and the assassin of President William McKinley. Czolgosz was born in Detroit to Polish parents in 1873. Some claimed that he was born in Alpena, Michigan, but in prison, Czolgosz said he was born in Detroit. Various sources, including police documents, list his birthplace as Detroit, but to this day, sources don't agree on where he was born. Wherever he was born, he lived some childhood years in Detroit, until his family moved to Cleveland.

In Cleveland in 1893, as a young adult, he worked in a wire mill. Due to the suffering national economy, the plant was shut down, and the workers were told that they would have to take a pay cut. That resulted in a strike, after which Czolgosz was fired and blacklisted, though he managed to get his job back the following year using a different name, Fred Nieman. (The Polish/German surname translates as "nobody.") The experience embittered him, and he increasingly focused on inequality between the wealthy and workers. In 1898, he quit his job—some claim he had a nervous breakdown—and settled on the family's farm. Over the next several years, Czolgosz spent much of his time reading radical works, and he reportedly developed a fascination with Italian anarchist Gaetano Bresci, who fatally shot Umberto I of Italy over the king's repressive policies—an event that made headlines around the world.

In 1901, Czolgosz became more involved in the anarchist movement, meeting Emma Goldman, a nationally famous radical anarchist, at a speech she gave in Cleveland. However, he used his assumed name, Fred Nieman, when he met her. In the summer of 1901, Czolgosz moved to Buffalo, New York, which was hosting the Pan-American Exposition.

On September 6, President McKinley was at the expo's Temple of Music to shake hands with voters, something he did without protection. Czolgosz attended, carrying a revolver he had concealed under a handkerchief when he stood in line to meet McKinley. When it was his turn in the receiving line, he shot McKinley twice at point-blank range in full view of shocked onlookers. The president died on September 14, 1901. Czolgosz was wrestled to the ground, immediately arrested and soon thereafter confessed to the crime: "I killed President McKinley because I done my duty. I didn't believe one man should have so much service, and another man should have none." He was initially thought to be part of a larger conspiring group, and several anarchists, including writer Emma Goldman, were briefly arrested. However, it was eventually determined that Czolgosz acted alone. His trial began on September 23, 1901, during which the judge rejected his attempt to plead guilty. The proceedings lasted just eight hours, and the defense attorneys—whom Czolgosz refused to help—called no witnesses. After only thirty minutes of deliberation, the jury found Czolgosz guilty, and he was given a death sentence.

He was later taken to Auburn State Prison in upstate New York, where he was confined to a "death cell." He was executed in the electric chair on October 29, 1901. Reportedly, his last words were, "I killed the president because he was the enemy of the good people—the working people. I am not sorry for the crime. I am sorry I could not see my father."

Czolgosz was buried in an unmarked grave on the grounds of the prison. Due to fears that his body might be stolen and celebrated as a martyr for anarchists around the world, his coffin was filled with sulfuric acid, causing the body to disintegrate.

The assassination of William McKinley in Buffalo triggered an instant furious hatred of anarchists. With Czolgosz's act, Americans became certain that laborers, immigrants and anarchy were linked and a source of evil. A great deal of time was spent by psychologists and medical doctors to determine if Czolgosz might be depressed, insane or subject to an uncontrollable impulse while he was incarcerated. This was not to try to get his sentence dropped for insanity but to try to understand why anyone would do such a thing knowing they would be caught and convicted. But they found no mental problems and found him to even be likeable to a degree. The doctor writing for the team examining Czolgosz reported, "As regards the existence of evidences of mental disease or defect, the result of the examinations was entirely negative. On the contrary, everything in his history as shown by his conduct and declarations points to him of the social disease—Anarchy, of which he was a victim.…His bearing and conduct from the time of the commission of the crime to his execution were entirely consistent with the teachings and creed of Anarchy."

This notion that anarchy is inherently evil and can corrupt a perfectly normal young American was suddenly picked up in the newspapers and by their readers. Anarchy was an infectious disease that had taken root in America and must be ripped out completely. In Detroit, an impromptu mass meeting of 1,500 people, including the mayor of Detroit, church leaders and state senators, gathered in the Light Guard Armory on September 14, 1901. The *Detroit Free Press* reported with headlines: "Detroiters Demand Suppression of Anarchists," "Kill them all! Cut them to pieces! Burn them! Some excited men shouted" and "Clergy of all denominations demand that now is the time to stamp the life out of anarchism."

This hysteria was not some out-of-control bloodlusting mob but the city's leaders. Deporting anarchists was not nearly enough. In speech after speech, ideas were put forth offering variations of rounding them up and arresting all anarchists and putting them in a ship to be sunk in the ocean. The Catholic Church demanded they be "stamped out."

The police arrested Jo Labadie, but he was defended by reporters on the scene and released.

The response from other anarchists in America was to scorn Czolgosz as too revolutionary. Despite this, Emma Goldman sympathized with the president's assassin. In her essay "The Tragedy in Buffalo," she wrote:

> *I did not know the man; no one as far as I am aware seems to have known him, but from his attitude and behavior so far, I feel that he was a soul in pain, a soul that could find no abode in this cruel world of ours.…As I write this my thoughts wander to the cell in Auburn, to the young man with the girlish face, about to be put to death by the coarse, brutal hands of the law, walking up and down the narrow cell, with cold, cruel eyes following him,*

"Who watch him when he tries to weep,
and when he tries to pray;
Who watch him lest himself should rob
The prison of its prey."

And my heart goes out to him in deep sympathy, and to all victims of a system of inequality, and the many who will die the forerunners of a better, nobler, grander life.

Despite the fear after McKinley's assassination, Socialism continued to grow in Michigan.

12

HANGING AT THE CLUB

THE GOLDEN AGE
OF FRATERNAL SOCIETIES

T hroughout Detroit, one can see old buildings with names on the front, sometimes carved in stone, such as "Odd Fellows Hall" downtown (now a Buffalo Wild Wings) or "Loyal Order of Moose Lodge" near the new Little Caesars Arena. Detroit is home to the largest Masonic Temple in the United States and the quirky castle-style five-story building on Grand River that was a former GAR club house.

These buildings are remnants from an era when 20 percent of adult American males belonged to a social club or two or five. In 1901, one in five men over the age of twenty-one belonged to multiple secret societies, as they were commonly called, whether they were clubs, fraternities, orders, mystical worlds, friendships, tabernacles, temples, nests, lodges, hives, tents, aeries, covens or dens.

By the 1870s, men began founding and joining new clubs by the thousands from all levels of society; the sheer size of Detroit's Masonic Temple attests to the popularity of the movement. Immigrants were founding clubs, as were Black men. Women would not be left out either and created auxiliaries of men's clubs or founded new major sisterhoods. From the 1870s to the end of the 1920s, Americans' social lives centered on these clubs.

The Masons and the Odd Fellows

Prior to the Civil War, the United States had just two well-known fraternal societies: Freemasons and the Independent Order of Odd Fellows. Both organizations came to the United States from Britain.

The Odd Fellows began in Detroit in 1846. Along with its ceremonies and parades, it helped widows and orphans of members and performed charitable acts. Both Freemasons and Odd Fellows had limited memberships composed of society's elite, such as business leaders or military officers. They were secretive, with passwords and secret rituals, and strange, with exotic titles and costumes. This would have a profound influence on future groups. It would seem that many men in the nineteenth century felt excluded and wanted to belong to a club. One man in Copper Harbor, Michigan, would change it all.

Inventing the Knights of Pythias

Justus Henry Rathbone was born in 1839 in New York to a prominent family of preachers. His father enrolled him in college to study law, but part way through, Rathbone quit to follow his true calling—theater. It is reported that he loved drama and costumes; there are images of him in costume playing everything from Pocahontas to Shakespeare. One play made a deep impression—a contemporary dramatization of the Greek legend of Damon and Pythias. Essentially, it is the story of two young men who put their lives in jeopardy for the sake of friendship.

At twenty-two, Rathbone formed a traveling theater troupe, but while touring the Upper Peninsula of Michigan, the troupe folded. Rathbone was broke. He got a job teaching in Copper Harbor, which was a logging camp. To while away the long winter evenings, Rathbone began writing a secret ritual based on the play of Damon and Pythias. Rathbone was already a Mason, so he knew rituals. He also invented costumes, headdresses, swords and other exotic regalia that he was sure would entice men his age to join. He called his organization the Knights of Pythias.

Seven years later, in 1864, while a noncombat soldier during the Civil War, he and four friends recruited men in their twenties to join the new club. Rathbone claimed that during the war Secretary of State William Seward had heard about the Knights of Pythias and invited Rathbone to the State Department, where he presented the club to Seward and Abraham Lincoln

JUSTUS HENRY RATHBONE,
FOUNDER & PAST SUPREME CHANCELLOR OF THE ORDER OF KNIGHTS OF PYTHIAS.

BORN: AT DEERFIELD, N.Y, OCT. 29TH 1839.   DIED: AT LIMA, OHIO, DEC. 9TH 1889.

THE ONLY PORTRAIT OF THE FOUNDER AUTHORIZED BY HIMSELF.

Justus Henry Rathbone was the founder of the international fraternal order of the Knights of Pythias. *Public domain.*

in Seward's office under their sworn promise that they would not reveal the secret ceremony. Lincoln told him it was a good idea and was much needed to heal the nation after the Civil War was over. By the time the war ended in 1866, the Knights of Pythias had four lodges and 379 members. Through aggressive recruiting and eliminating the exclusivity of the Masons and Odd Fellows, it grew rapidly. By 1874, the Knights of Pythias had 100,000 members and 1 million by the turn of the twentieth century. It was the third-largest club in the United States.

THE AGE OF FRATERNAL SOCIETIES BEGINS

The success of the Knights of Pythias inspired others, and secret societies were founded by the hundreds. By the 1870s, so many clubs were active in Detroit that the Detroit newspapers ran weekly columns, such as Clubs and Societies and Fraternal Societies, to keep track of their activities. In 1896, one expert estimated that 5.4 million men were members of one or more of the 568 secret societies in the United States. By 1907, that figure had risen to 10.5 million members.

A typical example, Henry Komrofsky, was born in 1872, raised in Detroit and known throughout the city as Henry the Hatter, since he was in the clothing business. In a book featuring Detroit's business leaders, Clarence Burton wrote of Komrofsky's memberships, "Fraternally, he is with the Schiller Lodge [a Masonic Lodge for Germans], Damascus Commendary; and with the Mystic Shrine. He also belongs to the Independent Order of Odd Fellows, the Benevolent Protective Order of Elks, the Knights of Pythias, and the Loyal Order of Moose. He is also a member of the Yacht Club, Harmonie Club, and German Turnverein [a German gymnastics organization]."

Some societies that started more than one hundred years ago are still in existence today, such as the Benevolent and Protective Order of Elks and the Fraternal Order of the Eagles. Others didn't fare so well. Few can recall the Order of Chosen Friends, the Protective and Benevolent Order of Beavers, the Jolly Bachelors, Supreme Tribe of Ben Hur, the United Ancient Order of Druids, Improved Order of Deer or the Order of the Owls (whose "Sacred Nest" was in Rhode Island). A personal favorite that counted thousands of members was a branch of the Masons called the Mystic Order of the Veiled Prophets of the Enchanted Realm, a club based on practical jokes. Another group name was the Concatenated Order of Hoo-Hoo, a peculiar name for men in the forestry product industry. Detroit clubs could be founded on anything, such as the Odd Experience Club, founded in 1895, which gathered to discuss, unsurprisingly, odd experiences. In 1910, the Church of New Thought had 125 members to promote positive thinking and optimism. Some clubs were formed by immigrant groups, like the Polish American Falcons and the German Order of Harugari. Black people formed branches of existing clubs, like the Odd Fellows and GAR, and founded their own clubs, including the Twelve Knights and the Daughters of Tabor. Women joined in auxiliaries, like Daughters of Rebekah, Eastern Stars and Daughters of Ruth.

The Hard Work of Membership

This was a time when normal, common Detroit men and women spent hours of intense study memorizing arcane rules, passwords and exotic titles; one women's club, the Daughters of Mokanna, referred to their leader as Supreme Mighty Chosen One. She resided in the "Supreme Cauldron." People practiced secret handshakes and learned symbols, fictitious histories, greetings and special rituals. Some carried swords, daggers and bejeweled battle axes. They dressed in exotic costumes, antlered headdresses, turbans or fantasy military uniforms and argued passionately over the color of gloves or special plumes for hats.

Members paid for their own regalia, some costing hundreds of dollars, in addition to their dues, annual donations, fees and special fundraisers. Companies made millions specializing in accoutrements for clubs, such as Pettibone Brothers Regalia Manufacturers from Cincinnati.

An 1871 constitutional manual titled "First Digest of the Laws of the Supreme Lodge of the World of the Knights of Pythias" states that the following regalia is mandated:

> *Emblems of Official Rank—Shoulder Straps for Officers*
> *For Supreme Chancellors—Royal purple silk velvet, four inches long by two inches wide, bordered with three rows of corded embroidery in gold. The escutcheon or crest of the order at each end, globe in the center....In addition, three small silver stars, one at the center of the top and one on the right and left of the strap.*

In the same manual, it specified that "pages" carried battle axes and shield, "esquires" lance and shield, "knights" sword and shield and other officers only a sword.

WHEN RITUALS GO WRONG

Sometimes, the sacred rituals got dangerous. On July 24, 1913, the Loyal Order of Moose, founded in 1888 in Louisville, Kentucky, met with tragedy when two candidates for membership, Donald A. Kenny and Christopher Gustin, died during the initiation ceremony held at a Moose Lodge in Birmingham, Alabama. The two were made to stare at a burning red-hot brand of the Order's Moose emblem. They were then blindfolded and disrobed while wires from a large battery were taped to their legs. Then, after a few sacred words were whispered in their ears, the Moose emblem (not red hot) was jammed on their bare chests as the battery wires on their legs were turned on. The aim was evidently to make them believe that they were being branded. They both had heart attacks and died. The *New York Times* reported that the Moose organization was held liable, and the four men conducting the initiation were charged with manslaughter.

In 1916, during the Knights of Tabor's sacred ritual in Texas, an unlucky candidate at the altar, Smith Johnson, tripped on a carpeted stair step and impaled himself on the imperial ceremonial sword. He survived and then sued and won in the Texas Supreme Court in a widely publicized lawsuit.

DETROIT CLUB CATERS TO THE ELITE

Some local clubs founded in Detroit were focused more on charity than ceremony. Many others have long histories, both well-known and obscure, such as the Detroit Athletic Club, the Detroit Yacht Club and the secretive and exclusive Yondotego Club, a dinner club on Jefferson Avenue, which is still active. (*Yondotego* means "beautiful view" in Algonquin.)

However, in the 1880s, the club most likely to attract Detroit's elite was the Detroit Club, whose 1891 clubhouse still stands at 712 Cass Avenue, with the club again open to the public. Registered as a historic landmark, the four-story redbrick building, described as Romanesque Revival and Italian Renaissance, held four bowling alleys, a library, dining rooms large and small, a billiard parlor, a barbershop, a wine cellar, a café and on the fourth-floor private rooms for members to sleep it off. Its members were Detroit's Victorian elite: industrialists, lawyers, lumber magnates, real estate dealers, railroad men, politicians and later automotive millionaires.

The Detroit Club, private luxury for the city's elite. *Library of Congress.*

The list of dignitaries entertained at the club is impressive: Presidents Truman, Hoover and Franklin Roosevelt; Prince William of Sweden, Empress Zita of Austria and the Duke of Windsor; and Margaret Truman, Charles Lindbergh, Gene Tunney, Admiral Byrd, John D. Rockefeller and Edward G. Robinson.

The No. 1 Convention Destination

The great event that every loyal member eagerly prepared for was the national convention. So many groups chose Detroit for their convention that by 1916, Detroit was considered the number-one destination for conventions by the National Tourist Board. The Antlered Ones—the Benevolent and Protective Order of Elks (originally called the Jolly Corks)—came to Detroit by the thousands in 1910. As the *Detroit Free Press* headline declared: "Women of Elks Parties Are Most Enthusiastic in Keeping up with Husbands in Pleasures of Entertainment. Members of the Grand Lodge and their ladies were given a generous sample of why life is worth living in Detroit."

SHRINERS TAKE OVER THE CITY

Nobody's convention in Detroit could compare in size, color and overall weird mayhem to the Ancient Arabic Order of the Nobles of the Mystic Shrine, better known as the Shriners. In early June 1897, the Shriners held their annual convention in Detroit with 100,000 Shriners, wives and girlfriends. They mobbed the city. For most of the year, these conventioneers were responsible, sober and dedicated citizens from cities and tiny towns across the United States and Canada, but for a few days, all was cast aside. Wearing their signature red fezzes, they overflowed the hotels and established headquarters for Imperial Potentate Harrison Dingman at the Russell House Hotel. The Texas delegate brought its tarantula juice, delegates from Temple Zem Zem (Erie, Pennsylvania) poured out their Zem Zem Spirits and the Indiana temple offered its Wabash Water. The *Detroit Free Press* reported that the Mystic Shrine ladies also "drank of the limpid waters of mirth and ministrely" at the Empire Theatre as they watched the Monster Trolley Party clanging up Woodward Avenue.

The Army of Mystic Shriners whooped it up on trollies, steamboats, Belle Isle, the roof of the Majestic Building, hotel lobbies and even the trains that brought them to Detroit. They brought camels and elephants for the parade to cross the burning sands of the streets of Detroit. Two black bears were tied up in the lobby of the Hotel Cadillac, and one "noble" from the Jackson Temple carried a raccoon on his shoulder.

The Temple Murhat from Indianapolis brought its own camel and dressed it in red socks, blue trousers, a carmine blouse, crimson fez and yellow Turkish slippers. Revelers grabbed hold of long ropes and serpentined and careened through the lobbies of hotels in lines of drunken nobles. Beautiful dancing women entertained during banquets while wearing white silk. Locals offering the Shriners room and board got into the spirit of things. A Detroit woman put up a sign on her house reading, "Dinner ready! Camels' milk hot or cold. Fricasseed tarantula!"

One Shriner gave Michigan governor Hazen S. Pingree an exploding autograph book that made everyone but the governor laugh.

In short, a hilarious time was had by all. But all things must end, and soon, they exchanged souvenirs, planned for next year's convention in Dallas, packed up and headed to the trains. The *Detroit Free Press* lamented, "They have gone from the oasis of Detroit to their various homes."

What Was I Thinking?

The question many scholars asked then and continue to ponder today is why did so many people do this? What induced a normal adult to put on a purple general's uniform with a gold fur collar? A few reasons have been suggested. Some of the less colorful groups organized to pool finances for pension benefits or life insurance. Many joined groups to help others through charitable activities or common political causes. The General Federation of Women's Clubs (GFWC) was founded in 1890 based on "Progressive politics and doing good deeds." Other organizations, like the largest club at the time, the GAR, offered simple companionship with other Union veterans from the Civil War, a part of soldiering they missed. Both veterans and non-veterans also had a common love of military uniforms and parades to show them off. It was social elitism and business connections that drew members to the local Detroit Club.

Finally, many proper, buttoned-down Victorians held a fascination for the world of spirits, hypnotism, séances, magic and ancient cults. This fad seemed to carry into the popular allure of club secrecy, mystical ceremonies and shared fantasy that went on behind the walls of secret societies.

But that desire came to a sudden stop in the 1920s, as if someone had flicked on the lights and everyone collectively said, "That's enough," dropped their horned helmets and went home.

Most groups were not regulated and didn't followed any established accounting procedures, opening them to embezzlement and fraud, although groups with the word "Improved" in their title meant that they were regularly audited. Some clubs were unrealistic in their promises of benefits based on collected member dues that were frequently set at a rate that was too low. For many groups, though, it was simply that the members got old. Retirement money paid to elderly supreme chancellors outnumbered dues from younger cadets, and the clubs became insolvent.

Less Colorful, More Charitable

Fraternal clubs enjoyed a spike in membership in the 1950s, with a bit less exoticism, but today membership is dwindling. The Masons fell from about 4 million members in 1965 to 1.25 million in 2013, with its average member's age sixty-two. Others follow similar trends. Virtually all surviving clubs have community service as the linchpin of the organization and are international in their reach. The Kiwanis Club, founded in Detroit in 1915, raises $100 million every year for family programs and emphasizes volunteer work. The Lions Club is known for its support of eyesight programs. The Rotary Club, aimed at business professionals and community leaders, tackles a variety of community issues.

The Shriners also focus on charity work over their once raucous party image. In 2010, they even changed their name from the colorful Ancient Arabic Order of the Nobles of the Mystic Shrine to the respectable albeit somewhat corporate Shriners International. They still love parades but typically drive tiny motorized cars to bring awareness to their charitable causes, notably Shriners hospitals for children.

For better or worse, the passwords, secret codes and camel-riding while drinking Zum Zum Juice have been left in the past.

13

THE BLACK HAND SOCIETY
THAT WAS NOT A SOCIETY

Sicilian Murder Colony
The Black Hand in Detroit. It is a constant menace in the Italian colony
keeping its members in abject terror.
—Detroit Free Press, *1908*

The population of Italian immigrants in Detroit was never as large as it was in other American cities like New York, Boston or San Francisco. But an Italian born in France was among the French founders of Detroit in 1701. Alphonse de Tonty (Alphonso Tonti) was de Le Moth Cadillac's lieutenant and good friend. When Cadillac was removed from Detroit, Tonty was appointed commandant and governed from 1704 to 1706 and again led the outpost from 1717 to 1728, writing famously in 1702, "The ground is very good there for eventually building a large town." Tonty's brother, Henri de Tonty (Enrico Tonti) became famous as the navigator for LaSalle and accompanied LaSalle on the *Griffon* as they explored the Great Lakes and the Mississippi River.

In the first half of the nineteenth century, very few Italians came to the United States and the country did nothing to encourage them to do so. The first Italian in Detroit was recorded in 1855. Detroit is one of the few cities in the States that had Italians from different regions of the country. Italian immigration occurred in three periods. The first to come to Detroit were from Genoa. In the second period, people from Lombardy arrived, and in the third period came the Sicilians. The early Northern Italian immigrants settled downtown and later near Eastern Market around Rivard and Watson and Erskine Streets, while the Sicilians were south of that, from the east side of Woodward to Beaubien from the river to East Larned. This was the area referred to as Little Italy or the Sicilian Colony. Later, another Italian area developed north of Gratiot to Mack Avenue.

These areas grew rapidly. In 1895, there were under two thousand Italians living in Detroit. The newly appointed pastor of Detroit took a census of the Italians to see if there were enough people to merit building a Catholic church for Italians, and he found the population included sixty-two families of Lombards, fifty-four families of Genoese, sixty families of Sicilians, fourteen families of Neapolitans, eight families of Tuscans, nine families of Venetians. This totaled 1,733 individuals.

By 1907, twenty-five thousand Italians were living in Michigan, ten thousand in Detroit and ten thousand in Calumet, and the remainder scattered throughout the state. By 1914, eighteen thousand were in Detroit, and by 1918, thirty to thirty-five thousand Italians called Detroit home.

The image of Italians in the nineteenth century was one of poor people, mainly unskilled laborers who were picturesque, shy but friendly when talked to, generous, child loving and living in tight-knit neighborhoods. The notion of violence, vendettas and mafia-style executional killings began when Italians murdered the chief of police in New Orleans in 1890. The piers in New Orleans were run by two feuding groups of Italians in a politically violent city. The chief of police, David Hennessy, was gunned down when he got involved in the conflict. When the Italians were arrested, mobs broke into the jail and murdered twelve Italians in their cells and lynched two more outside the jail. This made headlines in newspapers across the nation. The *Los Angeles Times* on November 3, 1890, reported:

> *Chief Hennessy's Murder*
> *Only the level headedness of a few leading men has prevented the great city of New Orleans into the scene of a fierce riot, having for its object the extermination of the Italians. As it is the feeling against these foreign residents the most bitter.*

The article reported that as Hennessy lay dying in the street from massive gunshot wounds, his last whispered words were, "The Dagos did it."

While the title "Black Hand" was used by a violent Socialist group in Spain, the first mention of the Italian version of the Black Hand that began appearing in Detroit was in 1904, when reports of bombings, murder, kidnapping and beatings were coming out of New York City, the biggest enclave of Italians in the United States. Newspaper features began looking more closely at the Italian neighborhoods on Detroit's east side. And then, as if by contagion, it began occurring in Detroit.

Although the Black Hand "Society" was not a society any more than safecrackers or burglars were in a secret nationwide society, the methods, the perpetrators and the victims were always similar. Crudely written letters with poor handwriting and bad spelling and adorned with knives dripping blood and skulls and smoking pistols that demanded money—large sums, sometimes ludicrous sums—were mailed to small businesses owned by Sicilians. Ironically, the Italian name used by some suspects for the activity was the "Lo Giusto" or the Just. Detroit Italians of Northern Italian origins claimed to have never been bothered by the letters. But Sicilian bakers, barbers, shoemakers, saloon owners, fruit vendors, doctors, grocers and more did receive the letters, which terrified them, as they feared for themselves and their families, who were frequently identified by name in the letter. One, recorded in the *Detroit Free Press* on July 31, 1904, was addressed to a grocer, Poggioriale Ciro, on Elizabeth Street in 1904. He and his family lived in rooms behind the store:

> *Dear Ciro,*
> *For the last time if you don't send that $2,000 you will be blown in the air with your family....Our powerful hand will destroy you, your family and your money....It is either your money or your blood we are asking for. So, do not fail to take along what we ask.*

The *Free Press* continued with the story. A few days after the letter was received by Ciro, a state excise inspector named William Connolly was walking near Ciro's grocery at night when he saw four well-dressed young men walking away from the front of the store. An explosion occurred, and the concussion knocked him off his feet. The explosion was felt several blocks away at the police station and sent the police to the grocery on Elizabeth Street. The police saw that the front of the store was blown off. The children had been sleeping in the back rooms: Massimo, twelve; Vencenzo, ten; and Frank, one month. Plaster from the ceiling fell on them, which badly scared them, but they were generally all right. Ciro and his wife had been across the street at a neighbor's and panicked at the explosion that had blown out windows of houses on both sides of Elizabeth Street. One hundred people poured into the street from a tenement and other houses. Women screamed, and men armed themselves.

Police reported that the Black Hand:

1.   *Terrifies Italians so none dare testify,*
2.   *Keeps Italians from buying property lest they be suspected of having money and thus be "black handed"*
3.   *Causes banks to refuse loans on property in the Italian district,*
4.   *Kidnaps judges of election and through terror prevents identification of kidnappers, and*
5.   *Kidnaps young girls and forces them into marriage with young gangsters—then coerces the parents of the girl to support the unwilling bride and her gangster husband.*

Some simply packed up and moved back to Italy. Many paid if they could find the money. Some ignored the letters, and others decided to fight and face the consequences. However, almost nobody called the police. Of the thirty-three killed in 1914, seven were women, three of whom were beaten to death. One policeman was killed; the year before, nine policemen had been killed. Of the deaths, twenty-three were killed by shooting and four by knife. Four were beaten to death, and two lives were lost by a Black Hand "infernal machine," a dynamite bomb. The Black Hand signature weapon of choice was a sawed-off shotgun.

The Italian section of Detroit was now being called the Sicilian Murder Colony and the Bomb Colony in the newspapers. The reaction across Detroit from years of lurid newspaper articles with horrifying details must have been severe, as the newspapers used Detroit Police statistics to chastise the public for condemning all Italians in the city, at that time 11,800 people, for the criminal behavior of what the police estimated to be 200 Black Handers.

"The entire Italian colony in Detroit is being denounced as if in alliance to frustrate the laws of the country in which it is domiciled, and comment is frequently made of the difficulty of arresting criminals of Italian origin.… As a whole, in fact, the Italians are a strong addition to the city's people. Because a handful of them defy the law and band themselves together to escape penalties the high credit due the many others should not be withheld," reported the *Detroit Free Press* on January 5, 1910.

By 1913, record numbers of murders were occurring, and killings began to be regarded as rival gang feuds, as gang leaders like Vito and Salvatore Adamo were called mystery figures in the papers and gunned down on the lower east side by rivals, the Gianolla brothers.

THE GOOD KILLERS

By the 1920s, the Detroit Police had a Black Hand Squad. The police stated in its annual report of 1922: "There are thirteen Italian speaking officers on this [homicide] squad all of whom are familiar with the methods and schemes peculiar to the Italian criminal."

In the 1920s, the police were seeing that not all the attacks on Sicilians were committed by Detroiters. As reported in the *Detroit Free Press* on September 25, 1920, "A few months ago, a score of new faces appeared among Detroit's Sicilians. They came from Pittsburg, New York, Patterson, New Jersey and elsewhere. And with their coming began the relentless succession of assassinations."

The murders were done by Sicilians from elsewhere, and they involved a group called the "Good Killers." In 1921, the Good Killers were suspected of committing as many as 125 murders in New York, Detroit, Pittsburgh, Chicago, Buffalo and several cities in New Jersey. Over the previous four years, the Good Killers were said to have committed as many as 70 murders in Detroit between 1917 and 1921, but the numbers were difficult to know for sure.

In 1921, the chief of Detroit's Black Hand Squad, Lieutenant Bert McPherson, received a cable from New York that could lead to knowledge about unsolved murders in Detroit. McPherson went to New York to question a murder suspect supposedly connected to the Good Killers, a twenty-eight-year-old barber named Bartolo Fantana. Fantana began associating with the organization around 1913–14, when he lived in a Castellammarese colony in Detroit. Castellammare del Golfo is a city on the coast of Sicily of about fifteen thousand people. The city was named for a famous fortress castle on the sea. Families in Castellammare, such as the Buccellatos and Bonventre, battled each other for eighty years and beyond; blood feuds—vendettas—were passed down generation after generation. Gavin Maxwell, the Scottish author, claimed that in the early, 1950s, 80 percent of the male population of the Castellammare had spent time in prison and that 30 percent had committed murder.

Fantana knew of the Good Killers operatives in Detroit and linked them to murders in New York and Detroit. He talked about a secret burial ground in an open field at Gratiot and Seven Mile for gang victims. This burial ground idea was discredited by McPherson, but he believed Fantana's confession about the murders. The Good Killers was a group of fifteen men from families in Castellammare in Sicily whose job was to assassinate members

SECRET SOCIETIES IN DETROIT

of rival Castellammare gangs in America in a transatlantic warfare that had been going on for over a decade. Fontana linked the Good Killers to the Detroit killing of three Buscellato brothers, two Giannola brothers, father and son Pietro and Joseph Bosco, Luca Sarcona, Andrea Lacatto and later the killing of Mike Matisi.

The Black Hand used the U.S. postal service to deliver its letters of extortion, which meant the extortionists were committing a federal crime, and the federal government began prosecuting suspects who were then sent to federal prisons, such as Leavenworth. It has been said that these prosecutions and imprisonments pushed the criminals away from the crude antics of the Black Hand. The criminals turned to more sophisticated ventures of prostitution rings, booze smuggling, money laundering and murder for hire by the 1920s. It was the beginning of the mafia.

PART III.

TWENTIETH-CENTURY DETROIT

14

FRANKLIN STREET SETTLEMENT HOUSE

In 1880, 116,340 people were living in Detroit. Then as now, it had hungry and lonely children whose mothers worked long hours and had trouble providing for them. There were middle-class women who formed an organization called the Western Association, through which they started a nursery called the Western Creche. (The word *creche* is used at Christmastime to model the story of the birth of Jesus, but it is also a British word for a nursery where babies and children are cared for during the working day.) However, they quickly realized it wasn't enough, so they reincorporated in 1881 and formed the Detroit Day Nursery and Kindergarten Association. Two empty lots on Church Street in Corktown were donated to them, and Governor Russell A. Alger took an interest in the project and, in 1882, erected a brick building at the cost of $5,000. In 1883, it opened its doors. The nursery cared for fifty children, with the ability to accommodate one hundred. To remove the stigma of free handouts, parents were charged five cents per child per day for the services. The second year the nursery was open, it served 4,900 meals, and by 1888, it was serving 8,232 meals to sixty-five children. It also provided instructions for young mothers to care for their babies. The need was great, so they opened a second location on Franklin Street along the banks of the Detroit River between Chene and Joseph Campau. Here they built a larger building and opened with seventy-five children. At the time, this was a poor neighborhood of Romanian, Belgian and Syrian immigrants packed into ramshackle houses, as it was before the area turned into an industrial zone.

An economic depression occurred in 1893, and the nursery was forced to close both locations as donations dried up. As things began to recover, the city was changing. The neighborhood in Corktown where the building was located began to improve. The group felt the need for its services was not as crucial, so it closed that facility and made Franklin Street the center of interest. It changed the name of the facility to the Franklin Street Settlement House.

The word *settlement* referred to settlement houses, a progressive reformist movement popular in the 1880s to the 1920s. In 1913, there were 413 settlements in thirty-two states. By the 1920s, there were almost 500 settlement houses in the country.

The idea was to "settle" educated middle-class women in poor urban neighborhoods. The volunteers would live in the neighborhood, hoping to communicate in a friendly way and share knowledge and culture and alleviate the poverty of their low-income neighbors. The settlement houses provided services such as daycare, education and healthcare to improve the lives of the poor in these areas. The first, Toynbee Hall, was in the east end of London, England. An American woman named Jane Addams worked at Toynbee Hall and then returned to Chicago, her home, and started the first and most famous American settlement house, called Hull House, with Ellen Gates Starr on Chicago's Near West Side in 1889.

From 1890 to 1910, more than twelve million Europeans immigrated to the United States. They provided cheap factory labor, which was in high demand during the Victorian days. Many immigrants resided in crowded and disease-ridden neighborhoods, worked long hours and lived in severe poverty. Children often worked to help support the family. Jane Addams was a sociologist, suffragette, social worker, philosopher and, in the 1920s, a Nobel Peace Prize winner. She inspired many women and men in the United States to address this need in their cities through the concept of settlement.

In 1902, Jane Addams visited Franklin Street Settlement and gave a lecture. The *Detroit Free Press* wrote about it on March 18, 1902:

> *"We need to get back to the first idea, that of simply living in a poor neighborhood first and foremost.…It is the impulse, the spirit that makes the settlement."*
>
> *She had something to say to the young women who, wishing to assist in the work were unable to converse with the people they met in the settlements. "People study foreign languages, read stories of peasant life*

Above: Franklin Settlement House around 1937. *Public domain.*

Right: Jane Addams, founder of Hull House in Chicago. Internationally recognized developer of settlement houses across the United States. In 1920, she won the Nobel Peace Prize. *Library of Congress.*

in foreign countries in order to get an idea of these people, and they neglect going to the foreign quarters of their own cities....I understand there are a great many Poles in your city. I should like to know how many of you have ever talked face to face with these people, and asked them concerning their hopes and fears."

Another aspect of settlement was to help foreign-born neighbors Americanize. In 1903, Franklin Settlement fed fifty foreign-born kindergarteners a Thanksgiving dinner with turkey, cranberry dressing, pie and fruit and nuts. At other times, the children were guided by holding mock elections and were taught at length about democracy.

On the fun side of things, they were given a vacant lot adjacent to the settlement, which was turned into a playground. As one hundred kids teetered and swung and dug white sand, the *Detroit Free Press* reported, "The children who frequent this pleasure ground are those of the very poor of that locality. All are shabbily dressed and many of them are dirty and unkempt." Perhaps to address this issue the settlement added a children's bathhouse and laundry facilities for families in the basement of the building.

Franklin Street Settlement continued to expand, offering services for older children and young men and women. In 1903, it added a men's club and, in 1907, dedicated an addition to its building with a gymnasium, an adult clinic and a bathhouse, a not unimportant feature since most dwellings had no bathtubs or showers. It provided English reading classes for men and women as part of their Americanization. Girls and young women started classes and parties for women of foreign birth who were their age—primarily Italians, Romanians and Syrians "to get them out of their homes so they might share the progress that the young men were enjoying." They put on dramas and held dances "for large girls," not to make anyone feel self-conscious. They had so many interns and volunteer sociology students from University of Michigan that they had a room called the Ann Arbor room set aside for the students.

But working in poor neighborhoods had its dangers. In 1904, the settlement was infected with diphtheria and a five-year-old child went home seriously ill. She later died. Her three-year-old sister, also at the school, also became ill but survived. The entire school had to be fumigated by the city health department.

Despite setbacks, the Franklin Settlement continued to grow and expand services. In the annual report of 1915, the scope of its work was breathtaking:

Medical Clinic—5,233 cases
Dental Clinic—2,590 cases
Clinic worker calls in neighborhood—3,076 calls
English Classes Attendance—6,028 (six months)
Sewing, cooking, music attendance—1,841 (six months)
Gymnasium and club attendance—26,725 (winter only)
Playground—12,765 (summer only)
Nursery attendance—4,141
Kindergarten (Under board of Ed.)—8,045
Employment secured for women—547
*Advice, help and temporary financial assistance—5,000 (by Neighborhood
    Visitors)*

In total, in 1915, it assisted in some way seventy-seven thousand people.

By 1920, the Franklin Street Settlement reported that it worked with people from twenty-four different nationalities. One teacher had been giving sewing classes for nearly thirty years. And the demographics were changing. Syrians were moving out of the neighborhood and Black people were taking their houses; one-third of the sewing classes were taken by Black women. In this time, the first Black baby, George Patton, was cared for at the settlement. He would continue at the settlement until, as a young adult, he was invited to join the staff, where he remained for forty-seven years to become director of maintenance.

Romanians continued to immigrate to the neighborhood, but by the time the Great Depression hit in 1929, the neighborhood was rapidly industrializing. Franklin Street Settlement decided to move to a facility a mile north and quarter mile east. Edsel Ford and his wife purchased two lots at 3360 Charlevoix Street and donated the land to the settlement. In 1937, it moved, and since it was no longer on Franklin Street, the group changed the name to the Franklin Settlement Center. The facility was three times as big but immediately reached capacity and was seeing 4,100 people come through the doors per week.

It conducted fund drives throughout World War II and received letters of thanks from homesick soldiers who grew up at Franklin Settlement. Many of Detroit's famous names spent their youth at Franklin Settlement, including former mayor Coleman Young and U.S. congressman John Conyers. In 1982, at the 100th anniversary of the Franklin Settlement, the executive director at the time, Gerald Smith, said, "There were Romanians, Polish, blacks, Italians—you can't go anyplace in the city of Detroit without meeting someone who has history at the Franklin Settlement."

Sophie Wright was born in 1866 and became a gifted educator. The Sophie Wright School began in New Orleans in the late 1800s as a day school for girls and was later a night school for men. It grew to become one of the most respected schools in New Orleans. Through friends in Detroit, Sophie Wright opened a kindergarten off Woodward that later included clubs and a nursery. In 1923, it was incorporated as the Sophie Wright Settlement and, in 1937, moved to Mitchell Street, one of the poorest neighborhoods in Detroit. The United Fund, which was administered by United Community Services (UCS), was a major funding source for Franklin Settlement. It also administered the funds of the Sophie Wright Settlement. In the 1950s, the agencies began a ten-year study into the possible benefits of a merger between Franklin Settlement and Sophie Wright Settlement. A joint committee between the two settlements was established to study the merger and to ensure that it could improve services while permitting each settlement to retain its identity. UCS suggested a trial merger of two and a half years. The trial merger was such a success that the two agencies combined services in the fall of 1967. It now has eight branches throughout the city as well as the Franklin Wright summer camp in Lake Orion. The biggest facility on Charlevoix now has a gymnasium, bowling alley, auditorium, medical clinic and day care center that serves one thousand neighborhood residents.

15

THE WOMEN'S CITY CLUB

I n 1873, Frances Newberry Bagley organized the Detroit Women's Club, the first women's club in the city. Meetings were held in her house. Women's clubs flourished in the United States in the Victorian era. They were known for promoting progressive causes and had a direct influence on the progressive politics popular in large cities during that time. Their growing importance became particularly apparent in the years around World War I, as they played a vital role in organizing the domestic war effort and pushed through the Eighteenth (Prohibition) and Nineteenth (women's suffrage) Amendments. After these national victories, women's organizations in Detroit and throughout the United States flourished.

Founding

Frances Bagley was among the most respected and admired women in Detroit in the 1870s, '80s and '90s. She traveled extensively, including to Egypt, Greece and the Middle East, and had a scholarly knowledge of ancient religions, about which she lectured. She was a member of the English Society for the Promotion of Hellenic Study, the Archeological Institute of America, the Anthropological Society in Washington and the Egyptian Exploration Society. She was one of seven women selected to act as commissioners-at-large at the Women's Hall at the Columbia World's Fair in Chicago in 1893.

She was dedicated to the betterment of young women in Detroit. In 1855, she married John Jordan Bagley of Detroit, who became a popular two-term governor of Michigan. (Bagley Street in Detroit is named after him.) They lived in a large house on Macomb Street between Brush and Randolph, later moving to their towering mansion, which stood on Grand Circus Park for decades, until it was demolished in 1914.

The club began promoting activities to help young women and families who might be struggling. One of the first ideas was to hold a rummage sale, selling secondhand clothing to women. The newspapers, male writers in particular, were immediately critical. One headline ridiculed, "Some Ladies Propose to Start a Ridiculous Second Hand Store." Some members at the store were confronted by men claiming they were neglecting their housework and families for club activities. Then, a second idea caught on. It was called the Work Depository. The Work Depository was located at 121 Michigan Avenue at Cass Avenue above a drugstore. Mrs. Bagley announced its establishment in the *Free Press*: "The object of this Work Depository is to provide work for any who would rather work than beg."

Women of Detroit were asked to drop off or mail in garments or other household items, such as sheets, towels and handkerchiefs that needed to be repaired, either mended, darned, hemmed or knitted. Any and all women would be employed to do the work with "fair remuneration." Within the first year, they had helped 120 women, of which 80 were regulars. Fifty or more girls found regular employment as servants through the Work Depository.

Francis Bagley died in 1898, and the Women's Club of Detroit continued to add members steadily, until in 1919, it was decided to expand the club tenfold to form the new Detroit Women's City Club. City clubs were common in large U.S. cities, and Detroit wanted to model itself after clubs in Boston, New York, Chicago and Kansas City. It would be open across the state of Michigan. Its charter stated that it would provide an opportunity for women to meet other women with a common interest in the welfare of Detroit and the state of Michigan, it would create an open forum for leaders and others to discuss matters of public interest and it would build a clubhouse in downtown Detroit where women could meet informally. It planned to have three thousand women signed up by the fall of 1919, which happened. The group selected Mary Chase Perry Stratton, the founder of Pewabic Pottery, to oversee the building design. She hired her husband, William B. Stratton, as the architect to design the building to be completed by 1924.

Left: Bagley mansion on Grand Circus Park (now demolished). First home of the Women's City Club of Detroit. *Library of Congress*.

Below: Federation of Women's Clubs, Executive Committee of Detroit, 1920s. *Arthur J. Lacy Papers, Bentley Historical Library, University of Michigan*.

The building is located on Park Avenue at Elizabeth Street. It was strongly influenced by the then popular style of the Arts and Crafts movement, with hand-wrought ironwork and Pewabic Pottery tilework throughout, including the arched entranceway and the swimming pool.

The building included a restaurant (and later a bar), a food store and a recreation area that had a heated swimming pool. The upper floors were used for apartments offered to women who might have just moved to Detroit and needed a wholesome place to reside. The club offered classes and recreational programs and, by 1950, had grown to eight thousand members, the largest women's club in the world. Among those meeting regularly in the building were the League of Women Voters, the Musicians' League and the Women's National Farm and Garden Club; among the speakers it hosted were Jane Addams and Lillian Russell.

However, as more alternatives for women to socialize and connect grew, the club membership began to dwindle. In 1967, the club was accused of racial discrimination for not allowing Black women to participate. By 1974,

Women's City Club in Detroit. *Public domain.*

the club had become too small to justify the big building, and the Women's City Club moved to a new, smaller facility.

The building switched owners and, in 2017, was purchased by the Ilitch family, who owned Olympia Entertainment, for $5.85 million. In 2019, Olympia Entertainment announced that the building would be renovated as part of the new Olympia development, the District Detroit.

16

THE INVISIBLE EMPIRE TAKES OVER DETROIT IN THE 1920s

*In the two years prior to 1925, 90 percent of the new recruits to the Detroit
police force were southern whites, susceptible to Klan propaganda.
—Walter White, assistant secretary of the NAACP in 1925*

The question one asks is how did a southern-conceived secret
society of White protestants that used fear and extreme violence
to intimidate nonwhite people and non-Protestants gain such a
strong base in Michigan and Detroit in the 1920s? It's a valid question for
us today, as we have seen the rise of White supremacy, intolerance and rural
resentment across the nation.

According to Eastern Michigan University historian JoEllen McNergney
Vinyard, one should look back to World War I and the distrust and bitter
resentment people felt against German immigrants in America, which
soon broadened into distrust of all immigrants who were non-Protestant.
Detroit ramped up production to provide the United States with the soaring
need for the materials of war. European immigrants and southern Black
and White people poured into Detroit, and the city's population surged,
passing the population of rural Michigan counties. This took away the rural
political majority; for years, the Republicans held not only a majority in the
legislature, but also every seat in both the House and Senate were held by
Republicans. This was changing. In 1925, Wayne County gained seven seats
in the Michigan state legislature at the expense of other regions.

"The fact that the farm population of the United States is shrinking has become so familiar that it has lost its capacity to stir interest," reported the *Detroit Free Press* on June 14, 1923.

This engendered groups like the Public-School Defense League. It started a campaign for the end of parochial schools, where children were taught by nuns in German and Polish. It sought to force all children to attend public schools and conform by becoming more American. Temperance and later Prohibition, greatly popular in rural Michigan, was also the product of White Protestants, "native Americans" (born in the United States with parents who were also born in the United States), and in part began as a way to control and change immigrant groups, since it was Germans and other immigrants who brewed beer and socialized in saloons.

In 1917, when the Bolsheviks took control of Russia and pulled out of the war with Germany, the fear of Socialism and Russian-style revolution in America took over the fear of Germans after World War I. Federal raids called Red Raids were developed by a young J. Edgar Hoover. In these, federal agents swooped down in Detroit and arrested hundreds of German and Polish immigrant men and held them in makeshift prisons in the downtown Detroit Federal Building. They released those who claimed U.S. citizenship and were eventually forced to release all of the men. The optimism of the "melting pot" of America was dropped for the use of fear to "Americanize the foreign element," as one pastor put it. Instead of promoting democracy around the world, many Americans now felt the need to protect democracy at home.

With the loss of political power and deep fear of losing a way of life, Michigan became fertile ground for the Ku Klux Klan, so-called guardians of "true America." Every county in the lower peninsula of Michigan had a Klavern (local Klan lodge). Members paid a ten-dollar fee and were handed a free white robe and mask. Vinyard wrote, "Atlanta based Klan Officials recorded more members in Michigan than any state in the South, and placed Michigan variously seventh or eighth nationally." But how did the Ku Klux Klan gain so much popularity in Detroit, to the point of nearly electing a write-in KKK candidate mayor and actually electing KKK candidates as city council members?

THE RISE OF THE KLAN

The Ku Klux Klan began in the South at the end of the Civil War, during the Reconstruction era. This first version of the Klan was founded in Pulaski, Tennessee, on December 24, 1865, by six former officers of the Confederate army. It was a highly secretive organization that used lynching, flogging and extreme violence to terrify White northern leaders, and politically active Black people. In 1872, the federal government passed the Enforcement Acts to prosecute the Klan for acts of violence, and Klan membership declined.

The second rise of the KKK occurred in 1915 atop Stone Mountain, Georgia, and was led by William Joseph Simmons, a former small-town minister. It was modeled on the movie *The Birth of a Nation* and Simmons's conversations with elderly people who remembered the original Klan. Simmons took the title of emperor and imperial wizard. It was this second version of the Klan that wore white robes and tall conical hats (some rode horses dressed in white robes) and burned crosses at night (as in the movie). Unlike the original Klan, which was a structureless militia, Simmons's Klan resembled other popular fraternal men's clubs of the day, with local chapters (Klaverns), a ritual book (the Kloran), membership dues (Klecktoken), secret signs and passwords and a weird initiation ritual based on the Bible and plagiarized poetry. It also held inductions of new members (naturalizations) led by the Klan, usually on remote farms at night beneath burning crosses that provided the only light and staged massive parades through big and small cities. It promoted "America for real Americans," which meant the Klan welcomed only White Protestants who were Americans born to American-born parents.

It began cultivating Detroit's "manly men" for "naturalization" in Detroit in the summer of 1921, when the first KKK Kleagle (recruiter), C.H. Norton, arrived. He had little success until September, when the *New York World* did a thorough exposé on the Klan, bringing it national attention. It was published locally in the *Detroit Free Press*. The Klan ran a full-page advertisement in the *Free Press* in the form of a letter from Imperial Wizard William Joseph Simmons in Atlanta, Georgia, refuting all claims in the article about the violence the KKK was reportedly using. C.H. Norton also ran a separate advertisement in a Detroit weekly, which showed a hooded Klan rider on a rearing horse holding a torch to invite Detroit men to join the cause. It stated, "One hundred percent Americans are wanted. None others may apply."

That fall, the Detroit Klan reached three thousand new members. The president of the Detroit City Council, John C. Lodge, instructed city police to treat any Klan demonstrations as disturbing the peace. The Klan canceled its plan to march in the Thanksgiving Day parade.

Henry Ford had become an inspiration to many in the Klan. In 1920, his newspaper, the *Dearborn Independent*, began a seven-year diatribe against the "international Jewish Conspiracy," which Ford blamed for all social ills. Jews began accusing Ford of financially backing the Ku Klux Klan. On May 29, 1923, the *New York Times* reported that the Order of B'rith Abraham stated, "Be it resolved that this convention accuse Mr. Ford of being the financial backer of the hooded Ku Klux Klan who approves of their unpatriotic exploitation against the Jews, Catholics, negros and foreigners. Grand Master Morris M. Green of New York commented, 'We feel that Henry Ford is behind the Ku Klux Klan, that he is their sponsor, and we are glad to join our Catholic brethren in fighting him and the organization."

Ford repeatedly denied any connection to the Klan.

In the Midwest and Michigan, the Klan saw its purpose as the self-appointed enforcers of the law; it believed law enforcement agencies were lax or corrupt and that true Americans must take action during these dire times. Enforcing Prohibition was one of the KKK's most common crusades. Prohibition was passed overwhelmingly in rural areas of the state but was unpopular in Detroit. Detroit was considered "notoriously wet." In 1918, Michigan was officially "dry." Records of the Detroit Police Department show that arrests for drunkenness rose steadily year after year, with 6,590 in 1920 and 28,804 in 1928. The population saw significant increases, but the rate of arrests of drunks rose as well, with 6.0 per one thousand in 1920 to 19.6 per one thousand in 1928. All this was much to the apoplectic frustration of rural Protestant ministers who saw the lax Prohibition laws a characteristic of Catholics immigrants and incompetent, indifferent or corrupt enforcement.

In Detroit, there were illegal rumrunners and speakeasys, and alcohol was still easily acquired. Polish Hamtramck drew a lot of the Klan's attention, and it conducted regular raids on saloons and roadhouses with the full endorsement of Protestant ministers. Members saw Hamtramck as mostly Polish Catholics who drank all their earnings, refused to give up their language and obeyed only the pope.

But soon, the Klan's focus turned to racist issues. Before the Great Migration of Black people from the South, the group's hatred was toward Catholics, Jews and immigrants. The Black population soared in the 1920s,

KKK cross raising in
1925. *Library of Congress.*

from 5,741 in 1910 to 40,000 in 1920 to 80,000 in 1925, but there was not enough decent housing, and they were forced to live in three small wards assigned to them on the near east side in 1910. Crushed in this slum, they sought housing in White neighborhoods. Working- and middle-class neighborhoods were upset by what they saw as the loss of their tranquil streets. The result was that Detroit became the great stronghold of the Klan in Michigan, with half of its members living in Detroit. Membership grew in 1921, from 3,000 to 22,000 in 1923, and earned the Klan $76,000. (Making money was a big part of the Ku Klux Klan.) It was seen as a check against Black people, as well as Jews and Catholics. The Klan added more Kleagles, and membership rose to 32,000. It found a new headquarters on two floors and forty thousand square feet at 206 East Hancock Street.

The Klan softened its appeal by offering fireworks displays at outdoor muster rallies and holding "Ku Klux Klan Dancing Karnivals—An event you'll long remember" at the Palace Gardens in Detroit.

Invigorated with new confidence, the Klan mobilized to enter politics in Michigan and the city in 1923. On Election Day in November 1923, it set up a burning cross at the east entrance of city hall just before the polls closed, but in 1924, even more violence was anticipated. The Klan backed a gubernatorial candidate friendly to the group and targeted city council members hostile to them and what they considered their key issue in Michigan—a statewide amendment outlawing parochial schools. Its candidates were defeated, and the school proposal was clearly rejected by voters.

In 1924, due to serious illness, the Democratic mayor of Detroit at the time, Frank Ellsworth Doremus, resigned from office, and a special election was called. The Klan put up its candidate, an unknown lawyer named Charles Bowles, against a Catholic Democrat, John Smith, and Republican Joseph A. Martin. In the primary to determine the candidates, Bowles came in third and was dropped from the ballot, but he decided to run anyway as a write-in candidate. John Smith campaigned hard in east side Polish and German Catholic churches, like St. Stanislaus, warning that the city did not want to be known as the first big city to elect a Klan candidate for mayor.

The Saturday night before the election, the largest gathering of Detroit Klan members ever held met in a field outside of Dearborn Township. People began arriving at six o'clock under the glare of an enormous burning cross and thousands of car headlights. The crowd was estimated to be twenty-five to fifty thousand, but KKK sentries guarded the event against reporters and nonmembers. Instructions were provided on how to vote for the write-in candidate.

Over 300,000 voted, the heaviest turnout for an election in Detroit's history at that time, and despite being a write-in candidate, with the Klan get out the vote support, Bowles almost won. Had it not been for John Smith's supporters who invalidated fifteen thousand ballots for Bowles for "misspelling," he would have won. The *Detroit News* identified 120 variants of the Bowles write-ins, which were rejected. These included Chas. Bowles, Charles Boles, Charles Bouls, Charles Bowls, Ch. Bowles, Cha. Bowels, Charles S. Bowles, Bowles.

The news went nationwide as Americans were shocked at the Ku Klux Klan's success in the nation's fourth-largest city. However, 1924 marked the Klan's high point in politics. In a rematch Detroit mayoral election in 1925 with candidates Bowles and Smith, Smith beat Bowles pretty handily. But the Klan began to rally supporters and focus all efforts on the explosive issue of Black segregation. In 1925, a White Klan mob forced a Black surgeon at Grace Hospital, Dr. Alex Turner, to vacate his new home in a northern White section of Detroit. A few weeks later, James Fletcher was forced out of his home by a White mob. But the most famous incident occurred in September 1925, when Dr. Ossian Sweet bought a small home in a working-class neighborhood on Garland Street. White neighbors threw bricks, stones and bottles at the house. Tragedy occurred when Sweet's brother Henry, at the house at the time, shot and killed one of the neighbors in the mob. The police had provided no protection; nevertheless, they arrested the entire Sweet household and charged them with first-degree murder. The trial of Dr. Ossian Sweet drew national attention. Progressive judge Frank Murphy oversaw the trial. Sweet was

The 1930 Ku Klux Klan Detroit mayoral candidate Charles Bowles during a radio speech at Detroit radio station WWJ. Detroit News *records, Bentley Historical Library, University of Michigan.*

KKK cross burning in 1925. *Library of Congress.*

defended by the famous defense attorney from Chicago Clarence Darrow and was eventually acquitted.

While the Klan claimed no connection to the affair, it was accused by Mayor John Smith of clearly exploiting the events to increase membership. Its failure in politics in 1925 spelled the end of the Klan in the area, as candidates distanced themselves from the group, and Klan membership collapsed by half in 1926. By 1928, the Klan had dwindled to a few hundred members. With financial problems, loss of member dues and failed events (like an indoor circus) and infighting among leadership, the Ku Klux Klan closed the Wayne County Klavern No. 68 for good. It tried to reopen in 1939 and 1941 and was later blamed by some for starting a racial riot in 1943 that killed twenty-four people, but days of hooded marches and Klonvocations under burning crosses were over for good in Detroit.

17

REIGN OF THE FLATHEADS

Paul Poluszynski was born in Poland and changed his name to Paul Jaworski (many times spelled Jawarski) in America. In 1945, *Life Magazine* described Jaworski as the "Cherub of the Church Choir," a chubby child with an angelic voice who sang in an Orthodox Ukrainian church but who would grow up to become a gangster, a confessed killer of twenty-six men and a brazen thief who, with his Detroit gang, would bring in record hauls of loot fleeing in a hail of gunfire in the style of Humphrey Bogart or James Cagney bad guys.

Jaworski started early. As a teenager, he enlisted his brother and other boys from the church to form a gang. Jaworski and the others looted shops and stores in his small town of Butler, Pennsylvania. He relished the reputation of daredevil and was a strong leader even at a young age, but soon, he grew tired of childish petty theft and wanted to move up to adult-style gangster activity.

Jaworski and his Flathead gang started their activities in Detroit and Hamtramck in the early 1920s. The gang's name came from a police report that described Jaworski as having a flat head—a flat head that would end up being his undoing. The gang started out robbing saloons, but Jaworski, smart and always ambitious, studied where big money could be had. He decided that payroll transfers at large plants and companies offered a possibility. Payroll transfers that moved bags of cash from banks to factories using armored cars and armed guards was a relatively new process that had weak spots and vulnerabilities that Jaworski would exploit. He combined well-thought-through plans with violence and surprise that terrified the public.

According to the *Los Angeles Times* on November 21, 1925, "A gang of five men tonight gained an $18,000 pay roll at the Ainsworth Manufacturing Company after a fight with two express messengers one of whom was killed and the other injured....A fusillade greeted the two messengers as they entered the factory and one of the robbers jerked the satchel from their hands and fled with two companions."

The two companions—Michael Konieczke, "Mickey the Pug," who lived on Yemens Avenue in Hamtramck, and Walter Makowski—were caught and convicted for the murder of the express messenger. Jaworski got away. In Detroit, he went by the alias of Paul Tapp. The gang moved from Detroit to Cleveland to Pittsburgh to New York, always keeping the police guessing and two steps behind them. Very soon, his picture was posted in Detroit with liberal rewards for his capture, so the group moved its activities to Pennsylvania.

The gang continued its violent payroll robbing spree. On December 24, 1925, it hit payday at the Pittsburgh Terminal Coal Company's coal mine number three in Cloverdale, Pennsylvania, killing the paymaster and getting away with $48,000. It was the first time the gang had robbed this company, and it would become important to Jaworski.

On March 11, 1927, supposedly the greatest year of the Jazz Age, Jaworkski and the Flathead gang pulled off a robbery that would make him infamous. It was the first gang to rob an armored truck. Payrolls had the additional advantage to robbers of not only offering huge amounts of cash, but also the armored car deliveries were very regular, occurring on the same day of the week and same hour of the day. Jaworski and the gang took over a Polish-born farm couple's remote cabin near the Cloverdale mine and began taking notes on the armored car's route—the exact time it passed on the roads and the highly armed escort who followed in a car behind the truck along the winding road that led to the mine. The pressure to capture the Flathead gang was growing, and the Pittsburgh police, along with the Pennsylvania State Police, began studying Jaworski's methods and hangouts.

Jaworski eventually knew the exact time that the armored truck with $100,000 in payroll would pass a specific location on the road. From the cabin, the gang could cut through a woodland to reach that spot on the road, unseen when lying down in a nearby hidden shallow pit. They spent a week digging a small tunnel beneath the road and then ran a wire to a gas pipe they had loaded with high explosives. They planted the gas pipe in the tunnel and waited. They contemplated the fact that the explosion would kill nine men in the armored truck, but worse for them was the possibility that the explosion would destroy or scatter the money across the countryside.

On an overcast day in March, they heard the truck coming up the lonely road, followed seventy-five feet behind by the unmarked guard car filled with five armed guards. Jaworski held the plunger to set off the explosion. As the truck neared the spot, he underestimated the speed of the car and set off the powder. It made an enormous explosion but caught the end of the truck, which was enough to send in into the air. The guard car drove full speed into the giant crater formed by the explosion, and the armored car fell back to the road and dropped on the guard car. None of the men in the vehicles moved and were assumed dead. (They were not; all the men lived.) The Brinks armored car was "open like a chicken crate."

The gang moved quickly and made off with a reported $104,834.38 of the Cloverdale mine payroll. The gang went back to the cabin and divided up the money. After that heist, armored truck builders switched from using wood floors to metal ones in their vehicles.

Every law enforcement agency in western Pennsylvania guarded streets and roads, knowing Jaworski and the gang were still in the countryside. Jaworski remained at the cabin while other gang members hunkered down in new hideouts. The area was heavily populated by Polish-born farmers, and the men knew the country very well. However, within twenty-four hours, the police had located Jaworski, who claimed he was just a visitor at the cabin. They arrested him, and soon he showed them his $40,000 take of the mine money.

He was put on trial in Pittsburgh and pleaded guilty to the dynamiting scheme. He was given a sentence of ten to twenty years in the federal penitentiary. At the same time, another gang member, Jack Vasbinder, was picked up. A month later, Jaworski was put on trial again for the brutal murder of the payroll master at the Cloverdale mine in the first robbery. In swift justice, he was found guilty and sentenced to be executed in the electric chair. Vasbinder was also found guilty of murder when he killed a man for not giving him a quarter.

Both Jaworski and Vasbinder were taken to the Pittsburgh jail, where their lawyers managed to get extensions for the executions. Then, on August 18, 1927, a visitor arrived for them. It was Jaworski's brother, Sam Pallas. As they talked, separated by an iron grill, Vasbinder stood nearby. Suddenly, Pallas pulled out two pistols and shot two guards. He forced another guard to open the cell and gave Jaworski and Vasbinder each a pistol. Then they shot their way out.

"Two convicted murderers, one a notorious Detroit gangster, shot their way to freedom this afternoon in one of the boldest dashes for liberty in the history of the Allegheny County jail," reported the *Detroit Free Press* on August 18, 1927.

Jaworski and Vasbinder moved from state to state with other gang members for over a year. Jaworski's home was in Detroit, and his wife still lived in the house. She was watched by police. Police intercepted letters she sent to Jaworski that were highly coded. He was wanted for murder in Detroit for the expressman killed at the Ainsworth factory robbery; however, Jaworski believed he was too much for the law and could never be stopped. On June 6, 1928, at eleven o'clock in the morning, he and six others managed to rob the payroll office of the *Detroit News*, bringing in guns hidden in paper bags. They walked up to the second-floor business offices of the *News* building on 615 West Lafayette Boulevard. On signal, bags were torn off and shotguns were pointed at employees, who stood in shocked disbelief as Jaworski and the others took $15,000. The first to arrive at the scene was a traffic cop, Sergeant George Barstad. The gang shot him dead on the stone steps leading

Business office of the *Detroit News*, where the Flathead Gang held a brutal armed robbery. Detroit News *records, Bentley Historical Library, University of Michigan.*

to the building. Another unsuspecting victim, an advertising salesman, was riddled with bullets as he approached the building.

Jaworski and Vasbinder escaped to Cleveland. In September 1928, the two were having lunch in a small Polish restaurant in Cleveland. The reward for Jaworski's capture was now $5,000. A man opened the door to the restaurant and quietly closed it again. He had spotted someone he knew from his childhood—the chubby kid from the boys' choir at the Ukrainian church—Paul Jaworski. He hid from the two men and called the police—money is money after all. He said he recognized his flat head. Within moments, the whole neighborhood was crowded with police blocking streets around the little restaurant on Fleet Street. Vasbinder suspected something, but Jaworski wasn't interested. When Vasbinder had the chance, he dashed out the back door of the restaurant. Jaworski then spotted the cops and pulled out his gun. He shot the first cop he saw and wounded a second in front of the restaurant, which gave him a moment of clearance. He ran to a house next door and tore up the stairs to the second floor, where he fired at police out the front and back windows. He eventually ran low on ammunition, and when the police threw smoke bombs through the windows, he made a dash out of a rear door, where he was met by a cop with a shotgun, who blasted him with slugs.

Although he was expected to die, he was tough and managed to live. After enough recovery, he was taken back to Pittsburgh and Pennsylvania's Rockview Penitentiary, where he confessed to over two dozen murders. On January 21, 1929, Jaworski was executed in the electric chair at the Rockview facility. He was buried on the prison grounds.

The other members of the Flathead gang were captured eventually, including Jaworski's brother in Detroit. One member escaped capture, Jack Vasbinder.

18

DETROIT'S PURPLES

During Prohibition in Detroit, it is said that there were over one hundred speakeasies and blind pigs in downtown alone. The Purple Gang hung out in clubs like the Clover Club, the Spot, the Town Pump, 1040 Club, Eddie's Hideaway and Boesky's Deli. In its heyday, the members were in their early twenties and dressed in expensive tailored suits and white Panama hats, which were popular in the 1920s. They were big spenders, but like other mobsters, they were vicious murderers. What made them different in Detroit was that they were Jewish, and they were predators of other gangs—a very dangerous strategy to take up. Members were never big enough to dominate an entire illicit industry, like Al Capone or Luciano. They preyed on small bootleggers and blind pigs but also the big Italian mobs, stealing or "hijacking," as it was called, illegal booze, kidnapping mob bosses and gamblers, busting up whorehouses and contract murdering others. When they first came on the scene, the police described them as suicidal. They got a lot of press, especially for two infamous mass shootings that kept big mobs out of Detroit, perhaps the most lucrative market in United States. At the height of Prohibition, bootlegging and illegal rumrunning booze from Canada, transporting and hiding it, distributing and selling it was said to employ fifty thousand people, and it was a $200 million industry. But for the Purples, their fame and their terrorist methods probably led to a short life. Their operations lasted from the mid-1920s to 1931, when they started to self-destruct and lost leaders to long-term prison sentences.

For all of the fame the Purples have received, the police estimated that there were only fifty-one total gang members, mostly from Detroit, but others were brought in for special jobs as the Purple Gang members became known to police. Of the fifty-one members, sixteen died violently and twenty-six served long prison terms.

They were the first native-born generation of Jews who came to Detroit from Europe at the turn of the twentieth century. There were thirty-five thousand Jews in Detroit by the 1920s. The gang members were sons of working-class parents, factory workers, street peddlers, scrap dealers and merchants—religiously conservative people whose children became doctors, judges, teachers and successful businessmen. The Purple Gang was an anomaly.

The two brothers who ran the gang, Abe and Raymond Bernstein, grew up with many of the gang members on the lower east side, from Jefferson Avenue to East Grand Boulevard along Hastings Street. Their father, Harry Bernstein, was a shoemaker from Poland who started and struggled in New York and then decided to try Detroit and arrived with his wife in 1902. As children, the Bernstein brothers and their compatriots were a street gang, shoplifting at candy stores and stealing fruit from vendors. They were wild boys who were a nuisance but whose crimes grew more serious, until the shop owners began to fear them. They were taken out of school due to incorrigible behavior and were transferred to the Bishop School, which handled problem children. At Bishop, classes were ungraded, and boys were taught industrial skills. It was here that they met other toughs who formed the original gang members, including the four Bernsteins brothers, Raymond, Abe, Joe and Izzy; three Fleisher brothers; Phillip and Harry Keywell; Abe Zussman; and others. The school actually became a rendezvous point for the gang, which would leave for the streets.

The gang got serious in the early 1920s, when the members began working for two men who were older than they were, Henry Shorr and Charlie Leiter, who operated a sugarhouse on Oakland Avenue. A sugarhouse was a business that supplied products needed to make alcohol for personal home consumption, something that was permitted in the Volstead Act during Prohibition. But of course, many of the customers were commercial businesses. The Oakland Sugar House supplied equipment, supplies like corn sugar and production knowhow to unlicensed bootleggers who sold illegal booze to blind pigs. It was a booming business. In his book *The Purple Gang*, Paul R. Kavieff wrote that in 1918, at the start of Prohibition, there were eight hundred unlicensed blind pigs in Detroit. By 1925, it was estimated there were between fifteen and twenty-five thousand blind pigs in the city. Shorr and Leiter also operated their own illegal production plants.

Joe Bernstein started working for the Sugar House Gang. When outside gangs were feuding violently and trying to take over the Oakland Sugar House, Shorr and Leiter hired the young future Purple Gang members, as well as mobsters from New York, for protection but also to extort money and hijack competitors' illegal booze. They started as bodyguards for Leiter and Shorr, as well as delivery truck drivers, where they would deliver corn sugar and other supplies to bootleggers. If while making a delivery they spotted finished bottles of alcohol, they would return with companions and steal the booze. On it went. The Oakland Sugar House Gang and the Purple Gang were made of the same men. The origin of the name Purple Gang is not known. It was suspected to come from retail shop owners in the gang's beginning, "They're off color like rotten beef—purple." But more likely, it was a catchy name made up by a newspaper reporter.

Down the street a few blocks north was the Oakland Health Club, a men-only Russian Jewish bathhouse where the gang members liked to hang out and sweat in the *banya* (a Russian Slavic version of a sauna). It was popular with Jewish businessmen and gangsters since they could talk freely in the banya—the men bathed naked, and there was no fear of concealed weapons or wires. Purple Gang members were known as the "boys" by other men at the bathhouse. The Oakland Health Club is now called the Schvitz (Yiddish for "sweat"). It was recently renovated and is open for business in the same location.

Things got very violent. In 1925, 232 homicides were reported in Detroit, including seven police officers killed while on duty. Fifty-three bodies were dragged from the Detroit River, and 6,453 arrests were made for Prohibition violators.

In 1925, along with the mayhem of illegal booze began what was called the Cleaners and Dyers War. It was started by a group of wholesale cleaners who wanted to boost (actually triple) the prices they charged to retail tailors and clothiers for cleaning and pressing men's suits. They decided they would begin an association and refused to sell to any retailer not in the association. They hired the Purple Gang at $1,000 per week to intimidate the retailers into joining the association. This proved to be a serious mistake. Honest businessmen were now being terrorized by ruthless mobsters. Two businesses were dynamited. When intimidation was turning into kidnapping and murder, the wholesalers tried to call off the Purple Gang. Sam Polakoff, the wholesalers' leader, was found dead in his car, his body riddled with bullets.

The group continued victimizing saloon and blind pig owners and regular businessmen. On March 17, 1928, the *Detroit Free Press* reported, "James E. Hall, wealthy beverage establishment owner who was kidnapped Friday and held for $10,000 ransom, was liberated today presumably after the demands of his abductors had been met....Police attributed the kidnapping to a band of gunmen known to them as 'the purple gang' which for several months has been preying on downtown saloon and blind pig owners."

The Purple Gang's biggest problem was that its activities were so violent that it received continuous press coverage and its fame spread. In 1927, one of the worst Purple Gang incidents occurred, called the Milaflores Massacre. People living in the Milaflores Apartment Building were rocked by massive gunfire in which three small-time unarmed gangsters were slaughtered by Purple Gang members. (This was the first time a Thompson submachine gun was used in a murder, which accounted for the massive destruction of the building's lobby. This led to an even more famous machine gun slaughter in Chicago, the St. Valentine's Day Massacre, which Purple Gang members were linked to.)

The final spectacular killing, which started the downfall of the Purple Gang, occurred in the early fall of 1931 at the Collingwood Manor, apartments on Collingwood Street near Rosa Parks Avenue. A month before the killing, members of the Purple Gang had rented an apartment in the quiet, respectable neighborhood. Ray Bernstein met an old friend from childhood days, Solly Levine, at the Boesky Deli. Levine was a small-time bookmaker. There were other Jewish gangs in the city. One of these, called the Little Jewish Navy, maintained a steady stream of nightly power boats to and from Canada for illegal booze. They were double-dealers with large debts and had burned the Purple Gang one too many times. Ray Bernstein knew that Solly Levine knew the members of the Little Jewish Navy and told him he wanted to cut a deal with them. He told Levine to bring the three leaders to a peaceful meeting to increase their volume of booze to the Purples for a national American Legion convention coming to Detroit. They were to meet on the second floor of the Collingwood Manor apartments. Levine agreed.

Levine and the three gang leaders reached the second floor of the building expecting a friendly meeting; instead, the Purples came out from behind a door and opened fire at the men. Each man was shot sixteen times. Solly Levine was unharmed as the men collapsed in a shower of bullets. The other gang members wanted to kill Levine, but Ray Bernstein held them back and said, "No, he's okay."

The Cadillac Hotel (now the Westin Book Cadillac Hotel), where Abe Bernstein lived for twenty-six years. He was found dead of a heart attack in 1968 in his residential room at the hotel. *Library of Congress.*

Levine was in a state of shock. The police learned of his connection to the killings and picked him up. He was an eyewitness and confessed, naming Bernstein and the others. Levine had a twelve-man guard of armed police with him when he was waiting for the trial. The court based on Levine's testimonial convicted the Purples, most importantly Ray Bernstein, who got life in prison. In prison, he liked to raise and train canaries to fly around his cell and take food from his hand. He would give the canaries as presents to old friends. His brother Abe, described as the brains of the gang, lived as a free man in the Cadillac Hotel in downtown Detroit for twenty-six years. He was described in a *New York Times* obituary as "a small and dapper man with the soft hands of a woman and a quiet way of speaking." He spent his life after his brother was sent to prison trying to get Ray's sentence commuted, convinced he was innocent. The sentence was commuted, but Ray soon died of cancer after leaving prison. Abe died of a heart attack in the hotel in 1968. He was seventy-six years old.

19

THE BLACK LEGION

SECRET TERROR OF THE 1930s

I will exert every possible means in my power for the extermination of anarchists, Communists, the Roman hierarchy and their abettors....Before violating a single clause or implied pledge of this, I will pray to an avenging God and unmerciful devil to tear my heart out and roast it over flames of sulfur. That my head be split open and my brains be scattered over the earth, that my body be ripped up, my bowels be torn out and fed to the carrion birds....And lastly may my soul be given unto torment; that my body be submerged into molten metal and stifled in the flames of hell, that that this punishment be meted out to me for all eternity in the name of God our creator. Amen.
—excerpt from the Black Legion oath

While the Ku Klux Klan had been popular and public in the 1920s in Detroit and across the United States, the Black Legion, whose members also wore hoods, although black not white, was secretive and unknown by almost all in the 1930s. The Black Legion was begun in Ohio in the 1920s by a former KKK member, Dr. Billy Shepard, who had been kicked out of the Klan. Shepard felt that the KKK had become dull and toothless; it lacked the excitement that the original southern KKK offered—the fear of the lawless nightriders. Shepard convinced a group of other KKK members to trade in their white robes with his black ones. The new group, which Shepard called the Black Guard, caused some trouble in eastern Ohio, but it died out. Shepard was then visited by Virgil "Bert" Effinger from Lima, Ohio. Effinger was also a former KKK member, and he convinced Shepard to partner with him and let him use Shepard's network of connections in the Klan to organize and expand the group. Shepard agreed and was eventually pushed out. Effinger was an electrician by trade and lived in a modest house in Lima with his wife and two daughters. While he claimed the organization was a national group, it was really limited to Michigan, eastern Ohio, Indiana and Illinois. And while he talked of millions of members, it was probably fewer than 200,000. Like past ultraconservative groups, the Black Legion railed against Catholics, Jews, Black people and most immigrants; however, the Black Legion's most venomous attacks were against Communists and labor unions. This made the members attractive to manufacturers who feared unionization in their plants. Henry Ford's notorious union buster, Harry Bennett, was suspected of using the Black Legion to target individuals. Unions and left-wing writers claimed the Black Legion was started by men like Henry Ford and Harry Bennett to destroy unions and demonize Communism.

The Black Legion was a more militaristic group, issuing guns almost immediately to new members. The club's motto was "Be Continually Armed." It recruited heavily from prison guards, police departments, sheriffs, the National Guard, rifle club members and even the FBI. It infiltrated many levels of government, including the courts and prosecutor's offices. One notorious member, Dayton Dean, claimed over one hundred officers of the Detroit police force were members.

The Black Legion used aggressive, sometimes brutal, methods to add members. It not only recruited men but also connived and sometimes kidnapped men who were then taken to night meetings in desolate rural locations or unlit basements. A recruit would be surrounded by members in black robes and hoods marked with white skull and crossbones. They pointed guns directly at the recruit's heart, and the recruit was forced to take the fearsome Black Oath. Few refused. Once they were signed members, they were given a bullet and told that if they said anything to anyone, they were to get a second bullet from a gun. (They were also known as the Bullet Club, the United Brotherhood, the Searchlight Club, Night Riders and more.) Once signed up, members were forced to attend meetings. Those who missed meetings were sometimes tied to a tree and flogged. If you questioned the action of superiors, you could be whipped. If you spoke to anyone about the group who was not a member, you could be flogged. The floggings were done before audiences to teach a lesson to all. Eight to twelve members would encircle the tied victim, and each would take a turn with the lash. It was excruciatingly painful and an ordeal from which some never recovered. Others watched in terror.

Effinger claimed that the group's object was protection and perpetuation of American ideals and social order, so along with kidnapping and assassinating labor leaders or newspaper editors with left-wing ideology, they might kidnap a man because he was suspected of beating his wife. He would be flogged. Many members were simply hardcore racists who enjoyed shooting and killing Black men. Sometimes innocent men were picked off the street at night and shot for the fun of it and then their bodies were dumped in rural ponds. One state police captain, Ira Marmon, claimed as many as fifty reported suicides were actually murders that had been committed in 1935 by the Black Legion.

THE MURDER OF CHARLES POOLE

By 1936, the police began to unravel the mystery of the Black Legion with the murder of Charles Poole. Poole was thirty-two years old with a one-year-old daughter and a wife soon to have another child. He was unemployed but a good man who loved his daughter and baseball, didn't drink too much and was friendly to most. His wife once dated a member of the Black Legion, Lowell Rushing, who hated Poole. At a Black Legion meeting, Rushing told Colonel Henry Davis, a leader of the group, about Charles Poole, a Catholic, who beat his pregnant wife, a Baptist, so badly that she had to hospitalized with broken bones and would have to give birth to a stillborn child. (She was actually in the hospital because she was giving birth to the baby, who was healthy, while Poole took care of the one-year-old at home.) The leader told Rushing's made-up story and worked the attendees to a frenzy, asking, "What are we going to do about this man?"

Davis, with four volunteers, met Poole and two of his friends at a bar. Davis told Poole that he was going to a meeting about amateur baseball. With two cars, Poole in the lead one, they headed out to a desolate spot between Detroit and Dearborn. They forced Poole out at gunpoint, and one of the members, Dayton Dean, shot Poole eight times with two pistols at point-blank range. Poole's body was rolled into the tall grass off Gulley Road.

The next morning, his body was discovered by a farm woman, and the Detroit Police began to investigate, along with a county sheriff. They took the dead man's fingerprints and, through the Associated Press's wire service, sent them to the Department of Justice in Washington, D.C. It promptly came back that they identified the murdered man as Charles Poole, whose name appeared in their files only because ten years ago, he had been arrested in Kansas for vagrancy. Detroit Police interviewed Poole's wife, who said he had gone out with friends, and she named them. The police located the friends, who told them of the group of four men who invited Poole to ride with them to a meeting about playing for a company's baseball team and getting a job. They gave descriptions of the men but not enough for police to identify them. Then a few days later one of Poole's friends spotted the leader of the group who'd abducted Poole. It was Harvey Davis.

They brought him in but got little out of him. One of the detectives attended Poole's funeral. He noticed one woman sitting alone and looking agitated. It was Lowell Rushing's sister Marcia. She was a friend of the Pooles. When the police questioned her, she said that she had made up the story about Poole beating his wife, as she knew her brother hated Poole.

Charles Poole's widow would spend her life defending Poole. In 1963, she wrote a letter to the editor at the *Detroit Free Press*, stating, "Charles Poole was never a wife beater and I should know because I was his wife. My husband was one of the best men who ever lived, so would you please stop saying that about him and let my dead husband rest in peace."

Marcia Rushing assumed that the Black Legion killed Poole and was now terrified they would come for her. The detective convinced her to give him a few names, and with those he arrested several members, including Dayton Dean, the executioner. Members, especially Dean, confessed and told the tale of the secretive club. Eventually, Dean confessed to killings and beatings and named others, which brought the secrets of the Black Legion into the light.

It was soon clear that the Black Legion had members in high places, including the police commissioner in Detroit, a county prosecutor and even a former Michigan governor. One of the names the Black Legion used was the Wolverine Republican Club. Michigan republicans were quick to deny affiliation with the vigilantes. Eventually, eleven former legion members were sentenced to prison for life.

Most of the Michigan Black Legion's leaders went to prison, but charges against Effinger, as well as twenty other defendants, were dropped because the prosecution was unable to "obtain the testimony of essential witnesses," according to an Associated Press story from May 18, 1939. The group's national leader, Virgil F. "Bert" Effinger, was fully acquitted and lived the rest of his life a free man.

20

NAZI SPY RINGS IN THE ARSENAL OF DEMOCRACY

I n the 1940s, Detroit converted tool and die shops, manufacturing plants, casting and forging facilities and assembly lines to become the largest supplier to the U.S. military. Plants halted the production of automobiles for civilian use and began rapidly producing Jeeps, M-5 tanks and B-24 bombers. By the summer of 1944, Ford's Willow Run plant cranked out one bomber an hour. No American city contributed more to the Allied powers during World War II than Detroit. As such, Detroit was of particular interest to the Germans. Detroiters became extremely watchful for spies and sabotage. Detroit's FBI in the 1930s converted from chasing down gangsters and smugglers to securing the city against espionage and protecting American technology. Between 1938 and 1939, the number of espionage cases handled by the FBI jumped 600 percent. The number of agents grew by similar ratios, from just 832 agents in 1939 to 4,600 by December 1943. It had one of its busiest years in 1942, arresting 56 people for espionage or failure to register as a foreign agent. In total, 120 homes of German and Italian aliens (non–U.S. citizens) were raided in Detroit, which produced a long list of items, some of which seem harmless today but in 1942 were illegal for them to possess, including shortwave radios, firearms, binoculars and cameras. The government established the Enemy Alien Board with wide-ranging powers to review and intern German, Italian and Japanese people.

Detroit had a large German-born population, so even before World War II, Nazis sought information on the manufacturing facilities in the city through Detroit residents. One man in particular, a Detroit restaurant owner and Nazi sympathizer, was caught helping a German POW who escaped from a Canadian camp. His name was Max Stephan, and he was found guilty of treason, the first U.S. citizen convicted of treason and sentenced to execution since the Whiskey Rebellion in 1794.

Since the middle of the nineteenth century, Germans had come to Detroit; in 1880, 28 percent of households in Detroit were headed by German immigrants. They clustered along industrial areas east of Woodward and along Gratiot Avenue, "walk to work" neighborhoods. These immigrants built churches and bought hundreds and hundreds of simple, small wood frame houses; Detroit had one of the highest percentages of single-family houses in the nation. They soon set up social clubs and halls, such as the Arbeiter Hall, where people could relax, speak German, sing the German songs they loved, talk politics and drink as they had done in the old country. The largest concentration of new immigrants to Detroit was around East Grand Boulevard and Jefferson Avenue, known at that time as Sauerkraut Row.

Many Germans came to Detroit and other cities in the United States during the chaos of the end of World War I in the 1920s and the severe economic depression in Germany in the early 1930s. So, when the fatherland began to pull itself back economically and then militarily from the humiliation of World War I and its aftermath, there was pride for some of the German population in Detroit and loyalties to America or Germany were often ambiguous. Even in the 1930s, Detroit had one of the largest pro-Nazi Bunds (alliance) in the Midwest—the Friends of New Germany. Author Arnie Berstein estimated the membership of the German Bunds in the United States was from ten to forty thousand.

The structure of the Bund was closely patterned after that of the Nazi Party in Germany. As the party had done in Germany, so did the Bund divide this country into *Gaus*, or districts, and *Ortegruppes* or units. Smaller subdivisions also followed the Nazi pattern. The various divisions of the Bund bore names identical with their counterparts in the Nazi organization. It adopted the official Nazi greeting, "Heil Hitler," later modified to "Heil"; such Nazi paraphernalia as the swastika; the Nazi salute; and the "Horst Wessel" song. The functions, uniforms and regulations of the various parts of the Bund were practically the same as those of the Nazi Party, and the holidays celebrated by the Nazi Party were compulsory days of celebration in the Bund, even the anniversary of the November 9 Beer Hall Putsch and the birthday of Adolf Hitler on April 10. Typical of its contempt for all things American, in its official calendar for the year 1937, July 4 is not listed as Independence Day but as the anniversary of the founding of the

D.K.V., or Deutscher Konsum Verband, the economic branch of the Bund whose function was to promote the sale of German goods and to boycott business operated by Jews in the United States.

Max Stephan's German restaurant at the corner of East Grand Boulevard and Jefferson Avenue was a gathering place for Bund activity. As World War II began, Stephan's restaurant was known for after midnight meetings for supporters of Adolf Hitler and the Nazi Party. It obviously had to be secretive. At the declaration of war in the United States, Stephan even had the word *German* crudely painted over on the sign of the restaurant.

Stephan was born in Germany in 1892 and served in the German army during the First World War. Following the defeat of Germany in 1918, Stephan left the army and was admitted

Detroit resident Max Stephan, who helped a German Luftwaffe lieutenant escape during World War II. *Author's collection.*

to the ranks of the German National Police. His military police duties as a prison guard served him well after the war, and later, he was hired as a civilian police officer in Cologne, which he held until 1924. He was offered a buyout, which he took and then he opened a beer hall in Cologne before immigrating with his wife, Agnes, to Canada and settling in Windsor, Ontario, in 1928. Prohibition was happening in the States, but not in Canada, where Max and Agnes Stephan opened a bar and restaurant with guest rooms above (actually a bordello run by Mrs. Stephan) to meet the demands of "tourists" from across the river. With the help of an American couple, the Stephans created falsified documents that allowed them to establish U.S. residency while living in Windsor.

When Prohibition ended, the Stephans moved to Detroit and opened their restaurant on East Jefferson Avenue. In 1935, they became U.S. citizens. The restaurant became a cultural hub for Germans in Detroit. It had a large room in the back that could hold 150 people. It was here that the Nazi sympathizers gathered at the start of World War II for late night meetings. Stephan hosted the night meetings of the Friends of New Germany, later growing to become the national German American Bund. The Bund, a nationwide body established in 1936 to foster national Socialism in America, envisioned itself as protecting the United States from Jewish Communist plots and Black cultural influences, such as jazz. The organization staged high-profile pro-Hitler rallies and hosted summer camps for youth in cities like Milwaukee. With a paramilitary wing, the Bund used intimidation against legitimate German cultural societies resistant to adopting Nazi ideology. Bund events were highly visible, attracting protestors and sometimes resulting in street violence.

One activity Stephan encouraged was for local German women to put together relief packages of candy, clothing, baked goods, tobacco and other necessities to mail to German POWs in Canadian camps, a legal activity even after war had been declared in the United States. Stephan got the prisoners' names from the German consulate in Detroit, which was run by a man who was also a Nazi sympathizer and knew Stephan well.

Of all the World War II POW camps in Canada, Bowmanville, northwest of Toronto, was among the nicest. The facility had been a reformatory for boys before the war and contained a gymnasium and a swimming pool. During World War II, Bowmanville was reopened as a camp for captured German officers. Nevertheless, as nice as it was, escape was always regarded as a military duty. While there was no established clandestine railroad to help escapees, prisoners arriving in late 1940 and early 1941 learned that they had friends in the United States, a country not yet at war with Germany.

Occasionally, the relief packages sent by the Detroit women would contain other articles hidden inside. These gifts included special inks, document paper and other materials that prisoners would use to forge selective-service cards, passports and identification to use during escapes. For this reason, the U.S. government required that packages carry return addresses. However, the prisoners at Bowmanville and other camps would save and memorize these addresses as a potential friendly contact in the States.

In 1940, the British captured Luftwaffe lieutenant Hans Peter Krug, a twenty-year-old officer in the German air force, after he was shot down during the Battle of Britain. Following hospitalization for a wounded hand and metal splinter in his eye, Krug was transferred to the Bowmanville POW camp. However, after a period of planning with his fellow officers, Krug made his escape from Bowmanville to Windsor, Ontario, by way of Toronto on April 15, 1942.

He walked north of Windsor for four miles along the river and stole a rowboat, improvising a paddle. He tried to use the red light atop the Penobscot Building as a guide, but due to the strait's strong current, Krug's rowboat was pushed off course and landed on Belle Isle. He crossed the

Belle Isle bridge at dawn. His first contact was Mrs. Margareta Bertelmann, whose return address was on his relief package. She lived in a modest house with her husband, Richard, and their small child over four miles due east up Jefferson Avenue, at 259 Philip Street, a few blocks from Alter Road and less than a mile to the border with Grosse Pointe. She and her husband had left Germany during the depression, and her husband had become a U.S. citizen while Margareta's citizenship was still pending.

She was home alone with her daughter when she heard a knock on the door at nine o'clock in the morning on Saturday April 18, 1942. A young man stood on the doorstep in dirty overalls and spoke in a heavy German accent. "I am from Canada—from Bowmanville," he said, showing her his golden officer epaulettes that he kept in his pocket.

She testified that she felt a shiver through her whole body, as she knew he was an escaped German prisoner of war. He was cold and "looked like a hunted animal," so she invited him inside. She offered him breakfast as he sat at her kitchen table. He said nothing. Terrified and unsure of what to do, she called Max Stephan. Stephan soon arrived in his car. Margareta guided him to Krug, and the heavyset Stephan sat across from him at the kitchen table as Krug told his story.

Stephan listened and then said, "Why don't you give yourself up? You haven't a chance."

"I have to try," Krug insisted.

Margareta listened, and when they both got up to leave, she gave Krug twenty dollars, a pair of shoes and fresh underwear.

Stephan took Krug to his restaurant on Jefferson Avenue and gave him food and drink. He then took him to get new clothes and a wallet. They drove downtown to a club called Haller's and several clubs after that, where they had drinks. Later, because it was the eve of Krug's twenty-second birthday, Stephan took him to a prostitute on Duffield Street, figuring he'd been a prisoner of war for two years, but Krug thought the offer crude and refused it. Stephan took him to a friend who owned the European Import Company, which sold imported German goods to homesick Germans. His friend was Theodore Donay. Donay was tall and had a cutlass scar on his cheek. He was a World War I veteran and one of Detroit's most fervid Hitler supporters. He listened to Krug and gave him twenty dollars out of sympathy. However, Donay's store clerk, Dietrich Rintelin, a German immigrant, called the FBI an hour later after Stephan and Krug had left the business.

On Sunday, Stephan bought Krug a bus ticket for Chicago, where Krug claimed he had another name from a relief package. He picked up Krug at the Field Hotel, where he had spent the night, got him on the bus and gave him twenty dollars as a parting gift. Krug thanked him as he left.

On Monday, the FBI arrested Max Stephan on the charge of harboring an alien fugitive, a charge that was soon changed to treason. Margareta Bertelmann, who was not a U.S. citizen, was arrested the same day and taken to immigration as an enemy alien.

The FBI learned that over the next thirteen days Krug had left Chicago and traveled by bus to cities across the United States and was heading to the Mexican border, where once in neutral Mexico, he would go to the German embassy in Mexico City and then return to Germany. The FBI sent notices and wanted posters to cities near the border. At a hotel in San Antonio, a hotel clerk had seen the FBI flier and noticed the similarity to the guest in one of the rooms. When the guest called the front desk and asked for a 7:00 a.m. wake-up call, the clerk noted his thick German accent and immediately called the San Antonio police. He was arrested in the hotel. The *Detroit Free Press* reported that Krug had two days of food rations, fresh clothing, a revolver, a handmade butcher knife, a map detailing his planned escape route and a list of hotels in Mexico City. In addition, there was a map identifying U.S. Army, Navy and Air Force bases; training camps; and fortifications. He also had a pair of golden epaulettes. Krug was arrogant in custody, refusing to be fingerprinted because he was an officer in the German Luftwaffe. He was fingerprinted anyway. He appeared in the newspapers in full military dress and in Germany was given a promotion for his exploits. Krug was extradited to Detroit.

Max Stephan remained in the Wayne County jail. With Krug captured, he thought it might go easier for him. He was released from his solitary jail cell on June 29, 1942, for his trial. He entered the courtroom, which was filled with spectators and faced U.S. district judge Arthur J. Tuttle.

Stephan's defense was weak; the FBI had been following him since he and his wife had moved to Detroit and knew about the after midnight pro-Nazi meetings at his restaurant and his activities supporting the Nazis and Germany. They even knew that he and his wife had committed fraud by declaring residency in Detroit when he was living in Windsor. The prosecution presented twenty witnesses, including Magareta Bertelmann, Theodore Donay, Donay's clerk Dietrich Rintelen and worst of all Oberleutnant Hans Peter Krug, who arrived in full dress uniform and knee-high polished boots. According to international law, Krug was not in any way compelled to testify for or against Stephan, but he did testify, much to the surprise of Stephan's dumbfounded defense lawyer, Verne

Amberson. There was speculation in the newspapers about why Krug decided to testify. One theory was that because of the honor code of a German Luftwaffe, Officer Krug felt he had to tell the truth no matter who it hurt. The other stronger argument was that the bumbling Stephan was stupid to help him, and Krug had contempt for the buffoon and his crude Detroit friends. Stephan had paraded Krug around Detroit like a trophy. Krug had no concern over what might happen to Stephan.

Amberson's defense focused on Stephan's intent. Stephan did not help Krug aid the German military in the war. He saw a young German man desperate and in need and acted to help him alone. It was not some planned plot against the United States. The U.S. prosecutor jumped on this hard, countering, "Was Krug playing hooky? Was Poor Max, Dumb Max, Generous Max helping a lonely desperate young man trying to get back to his mother and father?"

The resplendent Krug sitting in the courtroom in full uniform hardly looked desperate. The prosecutor pointed at Krug, saying, "That is an officer in Hitler's army! Part of the Luftwaffe that bombed innocent women and children in London. He came to Detroit to try and get back to Germany and back into a bomber where he could resume bombing and if he could, bomb the United States. Stephan tried to help him do this and that is why he is a traitor—a black hearted traitor!"

With the testimony over, Judge Tuttle reminded the jury that "if Stephan helped Krug, with the intention to help Germany, he is guilty. If the intent is absent, he is innocent."

Stephan sat waiting for the jury, six men and six women. After an hour and twenty-three minutes, they returned. Judge Tuttle called for the verdict. The foreman rose. The verdict was guilty.

On August 6, 1942, Stephan was back in court for the sentencing. Judge Tuttle addressed Stephan. "Do you have anything you wish to say before you hear your sentencing?"

Stephan rose, "I am not a traitor. And I am not afraid." He sat down, visibly shaking.

The court reviewed the evidence and activities of Stephan since his days in Canada. He was asked to stand to hear his sentence from Judge Tuttle: "The court does now here sentence the defendant, Max Stephan, to the custody of the United States marshal of the Eastern District of Michigan to be taken to the Federal Institution of Correction at Milan, Michigan and there confined in safe and secure custody until November 13, 1942. On that day within the walls of the Federal Correctional Institution, said defendant,

Front page headline of the *Detroit Times* during sentencing of Max Stephan, August 6, 1942. *Author's collection.*

Max Stephan, be by the United States marshal, hanged by the neck until Max Stephan is dead."

The spectators in the courtroom gasped, and one person clapped. Shaking almost uncontrollably, Stephan had difficulty walking as he was led out of the courtroom.

Returned to prison, Stephan had a new defense attorney, Nicolas Salowich. Salowich filed an appeal on the ruling, but it was rejected. Stephan's execution was pushed back to July 2, 1943. Salowich took Stephan's case to the U.S. Supreme Court, where the ruling was upheld. He returned to the Supreme Court eight times, but each time, he failed to get the ruling overturned. Out of options, Salowich, through U.S. Supreme Court justice Frank Murphy, appealed to the president of the United States, Franklin Roosevelt, for clemency. Others in Detroit also petitioned Roosevelt for mercy on Stephan. On July 1, 1943, the warden of the Milan prison, Cecil Shuttleworth, answered his telephone. It was a call from the director of prisons—Max Stephan would live. The president had commuted his sentence nine hours before he was scheduled to be hanged.

After confirming the call, Shuttleworth and Salowich went to Stephan's cell and gave him the news. Stephan was dumbfounded. They read him the text of the president's message: "The president has commuted the death sentence of Max Stephan of Detroit to imprisonment for the term of his natural life." The message went on to explain that there are different degrees of treason, as there are different qualities of murder. The president felt Stephan's treason was the parallel of murder in the second degree or manslaughter. The sentence was too severe.

A week later, Stephan was taken to the federal prison in Georgia. After eight years of imprisonment, Max Stephan's health began to fail, and he died of intestinal cancer. His wife, Agnes, regarded as an enemy alien, was deported to Germany at the end of the war. Stephan's friend Theodore Donay, owner of the European Import Company, was also convicted of treason. He lost his citizenship, his company was ruined and he served six years in federal prison. In 1950, he committed suicide while on a boat in the Pacific Ocean. Margareta Bertelmann went to prison for six years in New York. Once out, she filed for divorce from her husband, Richard, for neglect; he never once went to visit her in prison. Oberleutnant Hans Peter Krug was sent back to the POW camp in Canada and escaped again. This time he returned to Germany. In 1992, at age seventy-two, he was a retired steel salesman. When he was interviewed by the *Free Press*, he could remember the details of his escape and time in Detroit but none of his fear or emotions at the time.

21

A PHONY NAZI COUNTESS WOOED DETROIT

Another episode that brought World War II home to Detroiters in the summer of 1943 was hatched before the war was declared. A woman lived with her well-to-do family outside of Toronto in a town called Rosedale. Her Irish grandfather had made a fortune manufacturing men's hats. Her name was Grace Buchanan-Dineen. (She insisted her first name be pronounced "Grawce," rhyming with "moss." She also added the dash in her last name to look more continental. Buchanan was actually her middle name.) Buchanan-Dineen was educated at the Sacré Coeur Convent in Toulouse, France, until 1929. For the next nine years, she and her father resided in London, while her younger sister, Peg, remained in Toronto with their mother. In her twenties, Buchanan-Dineen traveled widely in Europe, a young lovely in the glamorous salons of Paris, Vienna and London, with men gathering round wherever she went. In the early winter of 1938, she and her father relocated to Budapest. He'd been suffering ill health for some time, and they chose the Hungarian capital for its many health springs. Despite some initial restorative benefits from the spas, Frank Dineen died that June.

In the spring of 1941, Buchanan-Dineen was approached by a Hungarian dancer named Sari de Hajek while she was living in Budapest. De Hajek was about the same age as Buchanan-Dineen. Described as lively and exuberant, De Hajek was a graduate of Vassar College. She had spent 1938 and 1939 in the United States as an exchange student and toured the States widely, giving lectures promoting Hungarian folk arts and dance, while her much

Grace Buchanan-Dineen. *Author's collection.*

older husband, Guyula Rozinek, worked in factories. The truth was that she toured with her husband, and they made contacts in the United States who might be useful as Nazi spies. In 1941, her husband was recognized as a German officer and was deported.

As they drew Buchanan-Dineen into their confidence, De Hajek told her that she had the beauty and well-bred manners to pull herself off in the United States as a member of aristocracy, a countess, who could give lectures on the hardships of life for women in war-torn Europe while collecting secrets from unsuspecting Americans. Buchanan-Dineen readily agreed.

Once she was approved for the new role, she was taken to a location in Germany to be trained in the espionage methods by the Gestapo. She would be paid $500 per month with a $2,500 advance; however, when war was declared, any transfer of funds from Germany to the United States was frozen, so Buchanan-Dineen never saw any money. On November 1, 1941, she was sent from Lisbon to Detroit. A year later, Germany and Japan declared war against the United States.

Detroit was becoming famous as the Arsenal of Democracy, and Buchanan-Dineen began her first lecture at the YWCA International Center and went on to prominent women's organizations such as the League of Catholic Women in Birmingham, drawing big crowds of wealthy Detroiters. She pretended to be the great-granddaughter of the last Count de Neen of Britany and spoke with a slight British accent. She was soon mingling with industrialist socialites to learn about manufacturing plants, industrial capacities and potential locations for sabotage or aerial bombing. She became prominent in Detroit society with her knowledge of European cities and her furs and jewelry.

Working her role as a countess but using her wealth as the granddaughter of a hat manufacturer, Buchanan-Dineen was an impeccable dresser and was wealthy but tasteful; her attire was frequently cited in the newspapers of the day. She was often seen in a mink coat, silver fox jacket or Persian lamb coat paired with hats, scarves, muffs and stoles of the same materials. Despite rationing for the war, her fashionable wardrobe included forty pairs of nylon hose and forty-one pairs of shoes. Her jewelry collection comprised twenty-seven rings set with diamonds and other precious stones, thirty-one bracelets, twenty-six pairs of earrings, three sets of pearls, three necklaces, three eighteen-karat gold watches and "more than two dozen lockets, pendants and other gewgaws of a similar nature." She took a prestigious address with an east side riverside apartment at 7716 East Jefferson Street, located next to Brodhead Naval Armory, near the Belle Isle bridge. Buchanan-Dineen's life was one of leisure, with nights out to dine at the city's night clubs or sipping sherry at parties she hosted at her apartment.

Soon in Detroit she was judging fashion shows, appearing on the radio and addressing the YWCA's charm school. Buchanan-Dineen entertained women's groups and societies with lectures describing what she called the "amusing side" of life in wartime Europe. Her standard topics included "Women in War Torn Europe," "Into the Light of Freedom" and "I Saw the Nazis in Central Europe," a subject J. Edgar Hoover, head of the FBI called "a gross understatement" during the war.

The spies in the inner circle included both men and women. A Nazi collaborator, Theresa Behrens, a friend of de Hajek, was a German Hungarian born in Yugoslavia. Her parents brought her to the United States as a teenager, and she was a naturalized citizen by the 1940s, although she planned to move back to Europe at the end of the war. She worked as a secretary at the International Center of the YWCA. She had set up Buchanan-Dineen's first lecture in Detroit. She was collecting information on the war work done at the Pullman company in Chicago. Behrens was avowedly and "violently pro-German" in outlook. "I am 100 per cent for Hitler," she once said of her long-standing views. "If Hitler wins, all those small countries in Europe will have their freedom." And she used her YWCA position to disseminate the Nazi ideology among the ethnic Germans she encountered, actively identifying and recruiting new sources for Buchanan-Dineen's ring.

Behrens put Buchanan-Dineen in contact with a friend, a well-respected obstetrician and surgeon named Fred William Thomas, who like Berens, lived in the East Village neighborhood in Detroit. He had an office in the Broderick Tower, then called the Eaton Tower. A native of Ohio, he went to the University of Michigan medical college and, after graduating, spent a year on exchange as a doctor in Hamburg, Germany.

Thomas was a rabid defender of Nazism. He was often a speaker at pro-Nazi rallies, he heckled Jewish speakers at events and a fiery speech given in 1939 at a German picnic caused him to be fired as a medical examiner with an insurance company. His own patients complained of his relentless harangues and arguments for Nazi beliefs, especially anti-Semitism. The visibility of Thomas at pro-Nazi rallies made him a known suspect to the FBI in Detroit for several years. Part of his role in the spy ring was to review Buchanan-Dineen's collected information and provide her prescriptions for hard-to-get chemicals, such as amendo pyrine used to make invisible ink. He was gathering information on the war work done at Westinghouse Electric's manufacturing plant in Ohio. He also had identified several plants in Ohio that were making nitroglycerin.

Another participant in the spy ring was Marianna Von Moltke, who unlike Buchanan-Dineen, was an actual countess; her husband, Count Henrich Von Moltke, was a descendent of a famous Prussian general, Count Helmuth Karl Bernhard Von Moltke. The tall, white-haired, dignified husband was a professor of German literature and language at Wayne University (now Wayne State University). They lived in a house near the campus, and his colleagues were surprised to learn that his wife was involved in Nazi activities, although FBI interviews with the countess quoted her as saying, "Hitler is the savior of the world." However, her role in the ring was always uncertain, and her husband was convinced that she was railroaded into a guilty plea made without legal counsel by the FBI.

Finally, the inner circle included Emma Elise and Carl John Wilhelm Leonhardt. A former officer in the German army, Carl had been among the founders of the Nazi movement in Detroit. His wife was known as "Mamma" to the rest of the spy ring and was, like Von Moltke, a German national. The group met in the basement of the couple's rooming house at 3521 Garland Avenue—just over two miles north of Buchanan-Dineen's apartment and a safe space where they could openly express their admiration of Nazi violence and racial superiority. The basement was decorated with swastikas and Nazi paraphernalia.

Each member of the group befriended workers in the defense plants for detailed information on innovations, production volumes, shipping volumes and locations in Europe, as well as weaknesses at the plants for sabotage. Buchanan-Dineen gathered their information and sent it on to Germany via letters. This information she wrote using toothpicks and invisible ink between the typed lines of innocent letters to fictitious friends.

They were mailed to a series of mail drops in neutral countries and then to Germany and the Nazis. The British Imperial Office of Censorship intercepted a letter from Germany to Buchanan-Dineen, which exposed the ring. It was forwarded to the FBI. At this time, Buchanan-Dineen's identity was still unknown. She was addressed only as Mrs. Smith.

A mail drop in Denmark was discovered by Ally spies, and one of Buchanan-Dineen's letters was passed onto the FBI. The FBI was quickly able to read the secret lines in the letter and, armed with only the postal code on the envelopes by interviewing postal carriers, zeroed in on the source of the letters. Agents held back, watched and waited to identify Buchanan-Dineen's accomplices. In March 1943, she took a trip to New York City. They trailed her and closed in.

They called on her in her New York hotel room and laid out their case. They knew it all, even her Canadian home and the phony countess role. Eventually, Buchanan-Dineen relented and quietly admitted to spying. The FBI told her that she faced a hard future locked up for years in prison or even the death penalty, but she could avoid that fate if she cooperated with them to help catch the others in the network. Her days of spying for the Nazis were done, and she agreed to be a counter agent.

In the meantime, the Germans wanted to speed up the information flow from Detroit, so Walter Abt, a Nazi agent who stayed at Leonhardt's rooming house in Detroit, wanted Buchanan-Dineen to use a shortwave radio to send her messages to the Germans from his farmhouse near Romeo, Michigan. The radio was not working, and Abt needed radio parts, but it was difficult to find them. Buying parts for a shortwave radio was too risky. The FBI kept a close watch on Abt and his farmhouse.

They also watched Dr. Thomas, Buchanan-Dineen's collaborator, using people to pose as patients in the doctor's home office. The FBI created a peephole from an adjacent apartment to Buchanan-Dineen's rooms and wired her apartment for sound. With that, they secretly recorded forty-one visits the doctor made to Buchanan-Dineen's apartment. They trailed Theresa Behrens and watched her pass along information to Buchanan-Dineen. The ring continued operating as it always had, but now the FBI reviewed all information the agents passed to Buchanan-Dineen while they provided her with harmless information developed by the U.S. War Department.

By midsummer, they had built a case against each member of the spy ring, and on August 24, 1943, they arrested Theresa Behrens in her home, along with the others and Buchanan-Dineen.

By early September, Buchanan-Dineen began testifying as the government's primary witness in a closed-door grand jury. She provided details on her role and the work of others in the plot. The grand jury's findings, reported on September 17, outlined forty-seven acts of espionage, stretching as far back as Sari de Hajek's husband's 1938 arrival in the States. Twenty-four people, both in the United States and overseas, committed these acts in Detroit and on foreign land. The six already in custody—Buchanan-Dineen, Behrens, Emma Leonhardt, Hoffman, Dr. Thomas and Von Moltke—were charged with conspiracy to collect and communicate to Germany information vital to "the national defense of the United States with intent to injure this country and to the advantage of the Nazi government." Just before the grand jury reported, Leonhardt's husband, as well as Walter Joseph Abt, were arrested. By the end of the same afternoon, they had both pleaded guilty to the same charges.

All of the defendants except American-born Dr. Thomas and Hoffman pleaded guilty without legal advice. Dr. Thomas's trial began in January 1944. Buchanan-Dineen was again the prosecution's primary witness, and she detailed over thirty meetings in his office, as well as many at her apartment, where he "compiled facts and provided information of such varied and complex nature she had to appear weekly at his office before transmitting it overseas."

On February 24, 1944, Dr. Thomas was declared guilty and sentenced to sixteen years in prison. Hoffman was declared unfit to stand trial.

The others were sentenced as well. Theresa Behrens received the harshest sentence of twenty years in prison. She collapsed after hearing the sentence. Carl Leonhardt and Walter Abt got ten years each. Emma Leonhardt got five years. Mariana Von Moltke's sentence was delayed because she claimed her guilty plea was coerced out of her by the FBI. Buchanan-Dineen, the ringleader, got twelve years in prison. Despite the fact that she acted as a counter-agent and primary witness, the court showed her no leniency. She later considered this a betrayal and said that she had expected a lighter sentence.

Waiting at the Wayne County jail for transfer to a federal prison, the spy ring's friendship evaporated. Behrens was furious, and her outrage echoed across the sixth floor of the lockup. "I wouldn't mind—," she screamed toward the others. "I wouldn't mind if I had done something to deserve this. I'm an American citizen, and they gave me 20 years and that skunk down there isn't a citizen and she gets 12 years."

Buchanan-Dineen served her sentence at the federal women's reformatory in Alderson, West Virginia. Arriving, she was concerned that she'd have to clean her own cell. Her sentence was reduced to nine years by President Harry Truman. She returned to Toronto.

The Von Moltkes' story ended sadly. After his wife's arrest, Professor Von Moltke was immediately dismissed from the Wayne State University faculty and had no money. He was convinced that his wife was guiltless and framed by the FBI. He hired a lawyer, Harry Okrent, who was Jewish.

Why would a Jew represent a Nazi spy? "Because a friend asked me to," he said. In 1932, Okrent had been a student of Heinrich Moltke's and had deep respect for the man, although he disagreed with some of his world views. "He was a marvelously inspiring teacher. A gentle soul," he said.

Von Moltke called Okrent and asked him to represent his wife in prison. "He said he had no job and no money and he had nowhere else to turn for help. I admired him. I couldn't turn the man down. I told him I would do it." He helped because of his friendship with Von Moltke and because he was convinced Marianna was innocent.

But it was a decision not without pain. "I had friends, good friends who forty years later still turn away when they see me. My mother was very troubled by it. It was the worst fight I ever had with her."

Okrent was not sure what Marianna Von Moltke was accused of. She had been implicated by Grace Buchanan-Dineen of passing information on to a mail drop in Switzerland. She would not budge from her claim that she was innocent, and the FBI insisted she was guilty. Eventually, the FBI told her it would lock up her husband if she didn't change her plea. That terrified her. She asked that if she pleaded guilty, they would not lock up her husband. They agreed, and eventually, she was sent to prison for four years. However, Okrent could not get her guilty plea overturned.

Heinrich Von Moltke changed his name to Miller, and Okrent got him a job filing books at a friend's business. When his wife was released from prison, the couple bought a candy shop on Kercheval at Beniteau Street but were eventually outed as former Nazi spies by a local preacher. They disappeared from Detroit, and by 1986, Okrent learned that they had died.

Interviewed in 1986, Okrent, living in an apartment in Southfield, had no problem with the decision he made in 1943. "I would make the same decision today," he said. "I do what I think is right. I do not toady to people."

22

THE COMMUNISTS

T he term *communism* was frequently used in the nineteenth century to describe actions or behaviors of social communes of any type. It was not until Karl Marx, assisted by Friedrich Engels, published the *Communist Manifesto* in 1848 that that would be changed. Communism started out as a tiny movement in London but caught on with a fury and raged across Europe, forever linking the word *communism* with Marxism. By 1950, nearly half the world's population was living under Marxist governments. The *Manifesto* opens with the dramatic words: "A spectre is haunting Europe—the spectre of communism," and ends by declaring, "The proletarians have nothing to lose but their chains. They have a world to win. Workers of the world, unite!"

The first American political party that was avowedly Marxist was the Workingmen's Party of the United States, founded in 1876. This party changed its name in 1877 to the Socialist Labor Party (SLP), and it recruited members throughout the United States, including Michigan.

On February 28, 1877, the *Washington Post* reported:

> *Communism Rampant*
> *(New York) A meeting of the four sections of the Socialist Party was held today and lasted for several hours. The room was decorated with National flags and the red flag of the Commune was prominently displayed....Isaac Bennet who was announced as belonging to the Workingman's Party made*

a long and highly inflammatory speech. In it he declared that both political parties were opposed to them, and if they wanted justice they must band together and make laws for themselves.

The SLP ran candidates in a number of municipal elections throughout the country, including elections in Detroit. The two leaders of the SLP in Michigan in the early days were Joseph Labadie of Detroit, who was also the city's prominent anarchist, and Judson Grenell of Ann Arbor. They became close friends. While never an anarchist, Grenell was a quiet man who fought for reforms all his life. Together, Labadie and Grenell founded the first national SLP publication, the weekly newspaper the *Detroit Socialist*, which ran from 1877 to 1878. They also wrote or edited the *Detroit Times* and the *Labor Review* (also known as *** *Three Stars*). In 1880, it published, "Labor Conquers Everything. Competition for the people is a system of extermination. Is the poor man a member of society or an enemy to it? We ask for an answer."

In 1901, the Socialist Party of America (SPA) was formed with dissidents from the SLP. In 1910, Victor Berger, one of the founding members of the SPA, became the first Socialist elected to the House of Representatives, representing Wisconsin's fifth congressional district, which encompassed Milwaukee. In Michigan during those two decades, several Michigan cities elected Socialist candidates. In 1911, SPA succeeded in electing Socialist mayors in Flint, Kalamazoo, Greenville, South Frankfort and Wilson, a tiny town in the Upper Peninsula. The SPA also had men run for mayor of Ann Arbor (1913) and Muskegon (1914). Later in 1916, a Socialist mayor was chosen in Traverse City. Other active Michigan Socialists in the early twentieth century were John Keracher of Detroit, a Scottish-born shoe merchant who joined the SPA in 1910 and founded the Proletarian University of Detroit, where he taught a course on Marx's *Das Kapital* to workers at night. Joseph Warnock of Harbor Springs was also a shoe merchant. He was elected president of the village of Harbor Springs in 1912 and ran for governor of Michigan in 1910, garnering 9,992 votes. Socialist newspapers across Michigan included *Tyomes* in Hancock (1903), the *Progressive Worker* in Holland (1911), *People's Paper* in Kalamazoo (1911) and the *Michigan Socialist* in Detroit (1916).

THE OCTOBER REVOLUTION CHANGED EVERYTHING

For the most part, people in Detroit and elsewhere in Michigan remained wary but tolerant of left-wing Socialists and anarchists, due to the 1886 anarchist bombings in Chicago, although police arrested participants at the Detroit May Day celebrations; in general, Detroiters felt they were immune to radical behavior that happened in other cities like New York, Cleveland and Chicago, which newspapers attributed to the strength and levelheaded thinking of the labor unions in the city. However, the Russian Revolution in 1917 and the 1918 threats from Lenin and Trotsky of a violent world Communist revolution produced backlash in western Europe and the United States. Americans such as journalist John Reed, who had been a Socialist, were witness to the revolution in Russia in September 1919. He wrote his experience in a book called *The October Revolution: Ten Days that Shook the World*. Reed formed a Bolshevik group, the Communist Party of America, with official recognition from the Comintern in Moscow. Other Socialists formed their versions of the Communist Party. Moscow pressured the various U.S. Communists to form one party, the Communist Party USA (CPUSA).

In 1918, the first version of the House Un-American Activities Committee was formed in the House of Representatives to investigate disloyalty, subversive activities and any U.S. private or public connections to Communism. It was called the Overman Committee after its leader, North Carolina senator Lee Slater Overman. His committee interviewed leaders of the defense department investigation who had already studied the behavior of the Bolsheviks' involvement in the United States. A Department of Defense official spoke to the committee, as reported in the *Christian Science Monitor* on January 24, 1919:

> *Through delegates to central councils, these agitators are extending their influence and their avowed aim is to take over our system of government....*
> *Money for purposes of propaganda and organizing is known to agents of our government to have come into the country.*
> *"Their idea is to overthrow this government?" queried Senator Overman.*
> *"Precisely," answered the witness.*

These investigations and aggression from the Russian Communist leadership triggered the first Red Scare and the Palmer Raids of 1920.

A. Mitchell Palmer was the attorney general under Woodrow Wilson. He initiated the raids, claiming to suppress and root out all left-wing political and labor radicals; Communists who were U.S. citizens would be jailed, and foreigners would be deported. Under his direction, in a massive operation, federal agents arrested thousands of alleged Communists and Socialists throughout the United States. The actions were characterized by exaggerated rhetoric, illegal search and seizures, false arrests and detentions and the deportation of several hundred suspected Communists and anarchists.

On the second day of January 1920 in Detroit, the Department of Justice agents were helped by 250 Detroit police officers and detectives, as well as 40 Michigan state police, and rounded up men and women suspected of being members of the Communist Party. At the time, there were about 5,000 Socialist Party members in Detroit. Repeated raids at the House of Masses, a meeting hall of the Socialists and Communists at Gratiot and St. Aubin Streets, was raided. Doors were kicked in, desks and furniture were smashed, all written material was confiscated and any person found in the building was arrested. Within seventy-two hours, they had arrested over 800 people. They were held in various police stations until transported in groups to the U.S. Federal Building in downtown Detroit for examination. They were held on the fifth floor in filthy makeshift confinements that offered only one bathroom for all of the prisoners. Anyone visiting them, such as families bringing food, were suspects, and some were detained. Arthur L. Barkley, head of the Department of Justice for Detroit, estimated that 280 of those arrested would face deportation. Those to be deported would be sent to Ellis Island in New York and then placed on one of three former U.S. Army troop transport ships that the newspapers nicknamed Soviet Arks.

Barkley was quoted in the *Detroit Free Press* on January 5, 1920, saying, "We have set out to rid Detroit of all men—or women for that matter—who preach the overthrow of the government by force….We believe these most recent raids and those conducted earlier in November have broken the back of Bolshevism in the city. In any event we are prepared to keep up the work until we have made a complete and lasting clean-up."

The Department of Justice claimed that the Communists planned to "bore from within" labor unions "by inciting simultaneous small strikes, to minor mass strikes, from minor mass strikes to general strikes, to national strikes to the dictatorship of the proletariat through revolution." Agents arrested men and women across the United States in cities like Des Moines, Portland, Oregon, Wichita, Toledo and Denver. In total, 2,743 people were held with a "perfect case" for deportation. The Department of Justice also claimed that there was $200 million in Russian gold to stop deportations, foment chaos and fund the revolution. A Michigan prosecuting attorney quoted in the newspapers claimed that mere membership in the Communist Party violated the State Criminal Syndicalism Act and subjected one person to the penalty of ten years in prison.

The hot rhetoric continued in April 1920 as J. Edgar Hoover predicted a bloody uprising on May Day. It never occurred. The Senate questioned the overreaching tactics of Palmer. He nevertheless sought the Democratic Party's nomination for president in 1920. In a crowded field of candidates, he presented himself as the most American of all. Campaigning during the Georgia primary, he said, "I am myself an American and I love to preach my doctrine before undiluted one hundred percent Americans, because my platform is, in a word, undiluted Americanism and undying loyalty to the republic." But labor and trade unions worked against his nomination, and he was passed over for president.

The CPUSA went in hiding and held secret meetings in places like Bridgeman, Michigan, at the Wulfskeel Resort.

Uproar over Communism seemed to increase in the 1930s and 1940s in Detroit. In 1933, Diego Rivera painted his magnificent frescos titled *Detroit Industry* in the garden court of the Detroit Institute of Arts (DIA). He was an open Communist, and the paintings, which he considered his greatest masterpieces, became a bitter controversy. They were threatened with destruction from conservatives who saw them as representing Communism and anti-Catholic church sentiments, particularly a panel that shows a mother with an infant being vaccinated by a doctor. Before the figures are farm animals, which provide a distinct reference to the manger scene of the New Testament. Edsel Ford had funded the artwork, and Rivera's work was strongly defended by Dr. D.W. Valentiner, director of the DIA, who claimed the paintings were simply the vision of a great artist.

The House investigations into Communist activity continued. The committee now called the House Un-American Activities Council (HUAC) was established in 1938. It was headed by Texas representative Martin Dies. Commonly, the committee was referred to as the Dies Committee. Claims were made with great publicity. On October 12, 1938, the *New York Times* reported, "Chester Howe investigator for the Dies Committee now sitting in Detroit, asserted today he would show that sit down strikes originated in Michigan were instigated by well-known communist agitators….He also charged that the wives of some of the most prominent agitators were teaching in Detroit schools and were forwarding the cause of un-Americanism to the children of the state."

Detroit factories were striking continually. From November 1936 to May 1937, there were 185 strikes in Detroit. The superintendent of Detroit Police claimed to the Dies Committee that 75 percent of the strikes were started by Communists and that Communist agitators now dominated the United Auto Workers Union, the schoolteachers of Detroit and the city health department.

The Detroit and state police began secretly gathering files on people suspected of having ties to left-wing political groups. They used spies and informants to gather information on what grew to 1.5 million files on people. The practice was finally abandoned as illegal in 1974. The FBI also used spies and informants. Perhaps the most famous was a small middle-aged woman who lived on East State Fair Street in Detroit and was twice divorced and without children. Her name was Bereniece Baldwin, but she was known commonly as Toby Baldwin. She had been a restaurant manager and a secretary, and at age forty-one, in 1943, through the encouragement of her then husband, she approached the FBI and was hired as an undercover agent to infiltrate the Communist Party in Detroit. In May 1943, she received her membership card and was given notice of a meeting to be held at 5643 Michigan Avenue, which she called "section 3 of branch 157." In about six months, she moved from that group to a newly formed group to serve members on the east side, called the Frederick Douglass Community Group. She moved from group to group frequently, as groups were formed and dissolved to avoid detection. Baldwin began as a steward, someone who collects dues and records meeting attendance, and after nine years, she became bookkeeper for the entire Detroit Communist Party. Quiet and innocuous, she must have seemed to be the most unlikely person to be an undercover agent, until the HUAC forum in Detroit.

The 1952, the HUAC forum came to Detroit. It was held on the seventh floor of the Federal Building in room 740. The forums were intended to generate high publicity, as they were jammed with newspaper reporters, and revelations made headlines across the country. The politicians relished the spotlight as the glorious guardians of America against the insidious red menace. Television was supposed to cover it, until for political reasons, that was squelched. Nevertheless, the committee was the talk of the town.

HUAC often pressured witnesses to surrender names and other information that could lead to the apprehension of Communists and Communist sympathizers. Committee members branded witnesses as "red" if they refused to comply or hesitated in answering committee questions. They seldom made arrests for Communist membership or agitation, as in this statement by Frank Tavenner during the hearing: "I want to state to you in advance of questioning you, that the members of the committee have not produced or presented any evidence of Communist Party membership. The purpose of asking you to come here is to inquire—into the activities of some of the organizations with which you have been connected, to see to what extent if any the committee should be interested in them from the standpoint of those manifesting communism."

Suspects could have a lawyer and could refuse to answer on the grounds of self-incrimination; however, that didn't matter, since the mere appearance as a suspect at the forum was enough to get one fired and destroy a life and a family. It left suspects with what the newspapers called "the Red tinge." This was beautifully depicted in Pulitzer Prize–winning author David Maraniss's book *A Good American Family*. Maraniss's father, Elliot Maraniss, had been an editor at the *Detroit Times* and a Communist. He was fired the moment he was named to appear before the committee in Detroit. It devasted him and his family in 1952.

COLEMAN YOUNG APPEARS BEFORE THE COMMITTEE

One encounter that went badly for the committee was the interrogation of Coleman Young, then thirty-four, whose confrontational aggressive appearance kept committee members flustered and off balance for over an hour and turned the inquiry away from Communism and into an accusatory confrontation on race. (The chairman of the committee, John S. Wood, and another committee member, Frank Tavenner, were both southerners. The HUAC was chaired and commonly included southern politicians, some with reputations as bigots.) Young's bold performance made him a local hero as a Black man who could stand up to White power, a reputation that would carry him to the state congress and later to become the first Black mayor of Detroit.

His exchanges with the committee, taken from the Congressional HUAC report, included:

> Mr. Tavenner: *You told us you were the executive secretary of the National Negro Congress—*
> Mr. Young: *The word is "Negro," not "Niggra."*
> Mr. Tavenner: *I said, "Negro." I think you are mistaken.*
> Mr. Young: *I hope I am. Speak more clearly.*

Mr. Wood: I will appreciate it if you will not argue with counsel.

Mr. Young: It isn't my purpose to argue. As a Negro I resent the slurring of the name of my race.

Mr. Wood: You are here for the purpose of answering questions.

Mr. Young: In some sections of the country they slur—

Mr. Tavenner: I am sorry. I didn't mean to slur it….

Mr. Wood: You are assuming what you don't know.

Mr. Young: You are assuming what I am going to say.

Mr. Wood: I want you to answer in what way the preamble of the National Negro Labor Council differs, if any, in respect to the National Negro Council.

Mr. Young: I would inform you, also, the word is "Negro."

Mr. Wood: I am sorry. If I made a different pronouncement of it, it is due to my inability to use the language any better than I do. I am trying to use it properly.

Mr. Young: It may be due to your southern background.

Mr. Wood: I am not ashamed of my southern background. For your information, out of the 112 Negro votes cast in the last election in the little village from which I come, I got 112 of them. That ought to be a complete answer of that. Now will you answer the question?

Mr. Young: You are through with that now, is that it?

Mr. Wood: I don't know.

Mr. Young: I happen to know in Georgia, Negro people are prevented from voting by virtue of terror, intimidation and lynchings. It is my contention that you would not be in Congress today were it not for the legal restrictions of voting on the part of my people.

Mr. Wood: That is a deliberate false statement on your part.

Mr. Young: My statement is in the record.

Mr. Wood: Mine, too.

Mr. Young: I will stand by my statement.

23

DRUM AND THE LEAGUE OF REVOLUTIONARY BLACK WORKERS

Dare to Fight! Dare to Win!
Fight, Fall, Fight Again, Fall Again—Fight on to Victory!
Long Live Black People in this Racist Land! Death to their Enemies!
Long Live the Heroic Black Worker's Struggle!
Long Live D.R.U.M.!

Even though Black people came to Detroit by the tens of thousands in the first few decades of the twentieth century, motivated in part by better jobs, they made up only 3 percent of the automotive workforce as late as 1940. It was the start of World War II that saw a sharp upturn in hiring Black men as plants converted to war production and ramped up need for more workers. There was a tremendous influx of new workers into the auto plants, including southerners and Black and White men and women. Black automotive workers jumped to 15 percent by 1945. They were drawn to plants close to where they lived, which meant the enormous old plants in the city of Detroit, such as the sixty-year-old Dodge Main (later known as Chrysler Hamtramck Assembly), Chrysler's Eldon Gear and Axel and the Ford River Rouge Complex.

Dodge Main was Chrysler's single biggest facility, at 4.48 million square feet. Chrysler bought it from Dodge in 1928. One out of every four cars Chrysler made came out of that plant. At its peak in the 1940s, forty thousand people worked at Dodge Main, but as various buildings that were part of Dodge Main became unneeded and were demolished, the number of workers fell steadily through the 1950s and 1960s, until the hourly workforce was at eight thousand.

On March 8, 1937, about ten thousand Dodge Main workers began a two-week sit-down strike to win company recognition of the United Automobile Workers (UAW). The strike, the largest sit-down in American history, involving sixty-three thousand employees, ended on March 25, and on April 7, the Chrysler Corporation recognized the union. It was a historic occasion in which a union that had been commonly found in local factories and shops organized an entire corporation. But over the years, for workers in the plant, especially young Black men, who by 1968 constituted 60 percent of the workers at Dodge Main, the UAW was viewed as a corporate entity—a corporate union more than a democratic union. Dodge Main, like other aged behemoth plants was old and very dangerous, with unsafe equipment maiming and sometimes killing workers. Racism was open between company foremen and union workers and between workers, as Polish workers from neighboring Hamtramck who had grown old in the plant clashed with young, impatient and severely frustrated Black men. The Black men were denied advancement in the plant and given the worst jobs, called HHD jobs, hot, heavy, dirty, while White workers became inspectors or advanced to skilled trades. Assembly line "speed ups" on the compact lines that produced Dodge Darts and Valiants were common and infuriated workers. During this time, speed went from forty-seven to sixty-two cars produced an hour. Illegal wildcat strikes were common. The tension at Dodge Main a year after the 1967 Detroit-wide race riots was explosive.

General Gordon Baker (General is his first name, not a rank; his friends called him Gen) was born in 1941 on Detroit's southwest side soon after his parents arrived from Augusta, Georgia. His father worked in at Midland Steel and then took a job at Chrysler. General Baker went to Southwestern High School in 1958 and, after graduation, searched for work in the automobile plants, but a recession kept him out of work until 1961, when he got a job at the Ford Motor's Foundry. While working at Ford, Baker attended classes at Highland Park Community College and Wayne State University, where he met likeminded students, like Luke Tripp, and cofounded an organization called UHURU ("freedom" in Swahili) in 1963. Around this time, he was arrested with others for booing the national anthem during a presentation of Detroit's bid for the Olympics held in downtown.

UHURU was a radical Black Power group that strongly believed and followed the African Independence movement, Malcom X and the Nation of Islam. In 1964, Baker and eighty-four other student activists went to Cuba

A 1968 General Baker demonstrating at Hamtramck Assembly Plant for DRUM. *Photo from government publication Extent of Subversion in the "New Left": Testimony of Robert J. Thomas [And Others] Hearings, Ninety-First Congress, Second Session."*

illegally for a visit, which had a profound influence on him. Among other things, he talked to Che Guevara and played baseball with Fidel Castro. He was supposed to go for two weeks but stayed on the sunny island for two months. Returning, he lost his job at the foundry, and in 1965, he joined a close friend, John Watson, to found the radical newspaper *Inner City Voice*. He was rejected by his draft board for military service, citing him as a security risk, and in 1966, he was arrested for carrying concealed weapons in his car, which he claimed he was planning to use to shoot police.

Eventually, Dodge Main began hiring. Baker said to the *Detroit Free Press* in 1986, "They flashed all the signs on Joseph Campau indicating that the employment office was open. They must have hired 3,000 to 4,000 employees at the same time, and the majority of the people they hired were young blacks. Most of the active people around DRUM all had the same history, age group, and background."

In 1968, a year after the rebellion had destroyed much of the city, Baker, now twenty-six years old, was working at Dodge Main. Baker said, "The rebellion of the streets had found its way to the plant gates." Baker began distributing *Inner City Voice* newspapers and confronting plant management and the UAW for racism and poor Black union representation, the close relationship of the union and the corporation and the plant conditions, especially the line speed-ups. On May 2, 1968, Baker and other Black and White workers called for a wildcat strike and, with four thousand people, closed the plant down. He and the others were fired, but while the White employees were rehired, Baker and a friend, Bennie Tate, were not. With John Watson, Mike Hamlin, Kenneth Cockrel, Luke Tripp and Chuck Wooten, Baker invited workers from Dodge Main to meet with them, and they formed DRUM, "Dodge Revolutionary Union Movement."

"It sounded good and it gave us a symbol," General Baker said to the *Detroit Free Press*.

DRUM members brought conga drums and marched to their beat as they picketed. "We set them on the curb. As a matter of fact, when we struck everybody was rockin'."

They distributed pamphlets with headlines stating, "Prepare for the Worst!" They refused to give pamphlets to "racist honkies" and divided Black workers by calling some "Uncle Tom traitors." Pamphlets had images of assault rifles on them, and at a fundraiser, prizes included a shotgun and an M1 carbine. Some picketers held signs that read, "Behead the Redhead," referring to UAW leader Walter Reuther.

On July 12, 1968, Baker staged another wildcat strike, which shut down the plant for two days. Two thousand picketers along the Joseph Campau side of the plant shut down the one line that produced Chargers and Barracudas. Some of the picketers were said to have carried weapons, such as bats and axe handles. The Detroit and Hamtramck police were called in. This was intense, especially after the rebellion of 1967, and the corporate executives were taking this seriously. The young White workers didn't like the group, and many of the older workers, Black and White, were afraid of them, according to a plant employee of the time.

"DRUM is headed by a heavyset man who calls himself General Baker. When he meets a visitor, he is flanked by two silent aides who stare sullenly from behind dark glasses," the *Wall Street Journal* reported in 1969.

DRUM demands were extreme and unrealistic:

Fifty Black foremen
Ten Black general foremen
Three Black superintendents
One Black plant manager
All Black doctors and 50 percent Black nurses in all medical facilities

50 percent Black security guards

No more union dues

A Black brother be appointed head of the Chrysler Board of Directors.

A committee of Black rank and file be set up to investigate racism by the
company and the union.

As Baker later explained, there seemed to be no point in moderation: "I
don't think any of the demands would be implemented. We didn't see any
give in either the union or the corporation."

The strike ended after two days, when DRUM withdrew. The model
caught on in other plants and produced ELRUM at the Eldon Avenue
Gear and Axle plant, FRUM Ford River Rouge complex, JARUM Chrysler
Jefferson Avenue Assembly Plant, CADRUM Cadillac Fleetwood Assembly
Plant, MARUM Mack Avenue Plant, MERUM Mound Road Engine
Plant, DRUM II Dodge Truck, UPRUM United Parcel Workers and even
NEWRUM *Detroit News* workers.

At the takeover of the Eldon Avenue Gear and Axle plant, one White
union worker, John Thomas, wrote about ELRUM: "They had started on
November 10, 1968. My first awareness of them was when they began
to put out leaflets. There was an immediate response, about 50 percent
positive and about 50 percent negative. The negative response came from
the older black workers and of course from the white workers, mainly
because the ELRUM language was harsh. They called people 'Toms,'
'Molly Toms,' 'Honky dogs,' 'pigs,' etc.…The older people had a problem
with the whole tone." Much later in an interview with Kenneth Cockrel, he
observed, "The movement might have benefited from a more sophisticated
public relations input."

DRUM also turned its pressure to UAW president Walter Reuther,
picketing UAW headquarters, Solidarity House. At the time, a spokesperson
for the UAW admitted that only seventy-five of the UAW's approximately
one thousand staffers were Black. Douglas Frazier was the UAW's man
in charge of Chrysler and was appointed by Reuther to handle the Black
militancy issues. While others were shocked and angered by DRUM's
threats of violence and obscene language, he was offended but noted that
the issues they were bringing up were real and that DRUM was sincere in
what it addressed.

LEAGUE OF REVOLUTIONARY BLACK WORKERS

To act in concert with DRUM's walkouts and disruptive activities, DRUM needed a support mechanism for legal, media and other resources. In June 1969, an organization was incorporated called the League of Revolutionary Black Workers and opened its headquarters on Cortland Street in Detroit.

The UAW attacked the league, sending letters to all 350,000 union members claiming the League of Revolutionary Black Workers was spreading terror in the plants. It accused "members of this so-called revolutionary group" of assaults and knifings. It suggested that they set fires in the plants. The UAW, it said, "will not protect members who resort to violence and intimidation with the conscious purpose of dividing our union along racial lines." Baker claimed the union never provided evidence of its charges. But the movement failed to attract a broad following, even among Black people. It never claimed more than one hundred members in the plant employing over ten thousand people.

Baker said one reason for DRUM's demise was that Black people had new remedies for discrimination. By 1971, the court had begun to make the Civil Rights Act a serious recourse; workers could appeal to the Equal Employment Opportunity Commission and the Michigan Civil Rights Commission.

The league leaders had formed into two camps on how to move forward and expand their successes. Kenneth Cockrel, Michael Hamlin and John Watson, who were Marxist-Leninists, believed they needed to include White people and others outside of Detroit to improve the capabilities of the organization and organize across the nation. They also wanted to include entities beyond the manufacturing plants in the movement, such as neighborhoods and schools. On the other side were General Baker, Chuck Wooten and John Williams, who wanted to keep a militant position and focus strictly on racism and Black workers at manufacturing plants in Detroit. The differences widened until August 23, 1971, when Cockrel, Watson and Hamlin resigned.

Later, Michael Hamlin wrote in *Detroit: I Do Mind Dying*, published nearly thirty years later, "People often ask me what the League's major weakness was.…The League had dizzying success. That caused us to lose sight of the limitations and capacities of our forces we had in place.…But at a certain point, I realized we were in deep water. We needed to shore up our forces. Our solution was to reach outside of Detroit and bring in talents that were needed and to reach out to other groups on the national scene with whom we had the most in common.…Some people didn't like outsiders coming on board."

24

BREAKTHROUGH AND THE OBSESSION OF ONE MAN

They say I see a communist under every bed. I tell you I do not. But I do check!
—Donald Lobsinger.

What happens to a person who spends an entire life consumed with one thing? Where everything and anything that comes to your attention is judged on a single issue—for or against Communism. Donald Lobsinger was such a man.

Lobsinger (he pronounced it LAWB-singer) was born in small house in Detroit on Drexel Street near Chandler Park in 1934, the son of a cleaner and a housekeeper. He attended Catholic schools, including DeLaSalle Collegiate High. He got a job with the City of Detroit Parks and Recreation Department, but in 1957, he was drafted into the army while taking college classes at University of Detroit and was sent to Germany. On a leave, he took a side trip out of uniform to Vienna, where he attended a world Communist youth conference, an open-air stadium with banners and balloons and released white doves arcing overhead. It changed his life. In an interview with Detroit Historical Society in 2016 he said:

> *I was in Vienna, Austria when a communist youth festival, sponsored by Moscow, was being held in Vienna. And the first time the soviets held their youth festival, their international youth festival, in a free country. They never did again after that because the Austrian students put up such resistance against that festival that the soviets never again held it in a free*

country. I met a number of those students. They knew I was an American soldier. I became friendly with them. My experience during that festival is what impacted my decision to fight the communists when I got out of the service.…That had such an effect on me that it lasted for at least two to three days, and I concluded communism is the wave of the future. The only way it will be defeated [is that it must be] *opposed by their enemies who have a greater dedication than they do.*

Lobsinger returned to Detroit in 1959 and resumed his job with the city while living with his parents. The extreme conservative movement in the United States was around in the 1950s and early 1960s, but it was splintered. The conspiracies in the 1930s and 1940s for Detroit's right-wing extremists focused on international Jewish plots, Socialism, international banks and Franklin Roosevelt, such as those espoused by the anti-Semitic Catholic priest Father Coughlin over the radio. The *Detroit Free Press*, in a summation of the fragmented character of the extreme right in the late 1950s and early 1960s, stated, "An assemblage of individuals more united by their opposition to things than their support.…The John Birch Society is the strongest star in this vague constellation. Around them swarm a hundred lesser bodies, some of them hardly visible through a telescope. Whenever these faint bodies are brought into view, they are found to consist of people—highly individualistic types who get together on occasion to discuss their common hatred of Communism, the United Nations or fluoridation."

Royal Rood was interviewed as one of these "lesser bodies." He was described as seventy years old sitting behind drawn blinds in gloomy isolation in "his small ill kept home on Cicotte Street" in Southwest Detroit at Michigan and Livernois. His hatred mainly focused on what society was doing wrong and included such things as the United Nations, fluoridation of the water, growing government, income tax and even the way American children were being taught reading in school. The *Detroit Free Press* reported on March 2, 1966, "Why did they stop children to read by phonetics? Do you know why? Well, the answer is that when children have to learn all these combinations of letters and can't sound them out with the aid of phonetics, reading becomes an unpleasant experience, they are held back, and they have trouble learning how to read. As semi-literates these children inevitably become the pawns of a coercive, encroaching government."

Lobsinger started attending John Birch Society meetings in Grosse Pointe Woods, home of Ed Kelly, where he met Kelly's brother Richard Kelly, who would become a member of Lobsinger's group, Breakthrough.

Twentieth-Century Detroit

Lobsinger viewed these Bircher gatherings as educational meetings, but he wanted action, so after nine months, he quit the Birchers. In 1960, at twenty-eight years old and a graduate student at Wayne State University, he began writing letters to the Wayne State governing board against lifting the ten-year ban on controversial speakers, a practice occurring at universities in Michigan and across the nation as the Red Scare began to subside. In 1961, with a thirty-two-year-old nurse named Ann Byerlein, he attended lectures at Wayne State given by people considered Communists, such as Herbert Aptheker from Columbia University. Apetheker's speech was screened beforehand, and he said nothing regarding Communism; his expertise was the history of Black people during the Civil War. Lobsinger was quoted in the *Detroit Free Press*, saying, "I don't care what he talked about, his very presence lends prestige to the Communists, and the fact that he was at Wayne University does too."

In 1963, Lobsinger founded an organization he called Breakthrough. Its purpose was to "break through the curtain of silence that has surrounded the communist conspiracy." When a *Free Press* interviewer asked Lobsinger about why his fear and hatred of Communism was so much more passionate than most people's, he answered, "with a special intensity," saying, "I am a firm believer in Christianity. I believe I have a moral obligation to fight communism because it is the greatest threat to everything I believe in.... There is an international communist conspiracy. I believe it has made inroads into every facet of society, including the government on a scale that is deeper than most Americans are able to recognize."

Breakthrough claimed to have one hundred to five hundred members. Its slogan was SASO, "Study, Arm, Store provisions, and Organize." Breakthrough's targets before the giant Vietnam War protest marches were Communist speakers at Wayne State University. Members also picketed the British consulate for the trade arrangements the British maintained with Communist North Vietnam. They protested the Moscow Chamber Orchestra when it played in Detroit, as well as the Bolshoi Ballet. They harassed the Soviet Union's national hockey team, which came to Detroit to play the Red Wings in a cultural exchange. (The Red Wings won.)

The Central Methodist Church on Woodward Avenue near Comerica Park, which was strongly against the war in Vietnam, received a lot of attention from Lobsinger and Breakthrough. "Earlier in the evening a handful of members from Breakthough, a right-wing organization interrupted the meeting by shouting 'traitor' and 'Communist' at speaker Ernest Goodman, a Detroit lawyer. The members were led by Donald

Donald Lobsinger throwing a Russian flag toward the speaker's platform at the Central Methodist Church to protest a seminar on the Vietnam war, 1966. At the right is Edward Kelly. *Author's collection.*

Lobsinger who tossed a red flag in front of the speakers' stage," reported the *Detroit Free Press* on December 29, 1966.

Lobsinger continued to live at his parents' home in Detroit and kept his clerk job with the City of Detroit, using his vacation time to stage activities and defend himself in court.

He directed much of his ultraconservative Catholic attack against liberal Catholics and Cardinal Dearden, who he accused of funding Black revolutionaries and other Communist groups. Antiwar priests, such as Thomas Gumbleton, he labeled traitors. He attacked abortion rights advocates and women's rights marchers. He hated Catholic "jazz masses." His publicity-seeking demonstrations, arrests and personal behavior were too much for conservative and moderate Republicans, who kept their distance from him. He considered Nixon and Kissinger too soft on Communism.

In his 2016 interview, Lobsinger said, "The 1960s were a communist-inspired revolution that overturned most of the values in this country. Black Lives Matter, groups like this. This is all communist inspired. You can go right back to the '60s, it's the same thing, same pattern, same slogans, same everything."

Donald Lobsinger got arrested in March 1966 for disturbing the peace with two other members of Breakthrough. At the time, the largest antiwar demonstration Detroit had ever seen started at Grand Circus Park and marched toward Campus Martius. Lobsinger and the other members of Breakthrough were accused of punching marchers and sticking them with hat pins. One marcher ripped a swastika pin off one member's shirt.

AFTER THE 1967 REBELLION A NEW DIRECTION

[The Detroit Riot] *deepened the fears of many whites even as it raised the militancy of many Negroes.*
—*Mel Ravitz, Detroit city councilman*

After the July 1967 rebellion, Lobsinger took on a new role. As University of Michigan history professor Sidney Fine wrote in his 2007 book *Violence in the Model City*, "Whereas Breakthrough had been able to attract only two or three hundred persons to its meetings before the riot, audiences many times larger than that appeared afterward." Lobsinger was interviewed by the Kerner Commission toward the end of 1967 and said that the purpose of Breakthrough was to "arm the whites" and help them stay in Detroit to prevent "guerilla warfare in the suburbs." In his view, the police had failed to protect the community. Lobsinger held meetings at places like the Flamingo Hall on East Seven Mile at Gratiot, where overflow crowds came to hear Lobsinger tell followers to buy weapons and certain supplies to store up for "the next much more terrifying riot." Breakthrough suggested that people arrange for locations where they could send their children. Lobsinger claimed that the riot had been a Communist-inspired insurrection. He advised White people, who Sidney Fine described as middle aged and "many of them of Eastern European extraction," to establish a block-by-block home defense system against armed terrorists invading from the inner city to "murder the men and rape the women." The National Rifle Association displayed weapons at the meetings.

As Lobsinger said, "Part of the reason we got people to come to these rallies in the numbers that we did was that in the neighborhoods surrounding the halls where we were holding the meetings, we saturated the neighborhoods with leaflets and flyers telling them, 'Will you be prepared for another riot if there is one?' And that's why people came. They came walking—it's unbelievable the response that we got to those leaflets."

Just as White people were preparing for the onslaught of Black people, the Black leadership was warning the Black community that police would provoke an incident as an excuse to attack them. John Watson's newsletter, *Inner City Voice*, warned in headlines, "Detroit's Concentration Camps Waiting for Blacks."

Lobsinger, interviewed much later, said, "I saw [the riot] as dry runs for the big push that would result in the takeover of the United States by the communists."

In 1969, Lobsinger and Breakthrough members protested the visit of Dr. Martin Luther King, who Lobsinger was convinced was a Communist. Three weeks before his death, King spoke at Grosse Pointe South High School in Grosse Pointe Farms. Lobsinger commented, "That's why we opposed Martin Luther King. Because Martin Luther King and his communist associations and his communist background, Martin Luther King was no patriot! He was an enemy of the United States! He supported the communists during the Vietnam War! And we had a huge demonstration outside Grosse Pointe High School in early 1968. And inside, too, to the point where Martin Luther King had a press conference the next day and said that never in his experience did he experience anything like this opposition at Grosse Pointe High School at an indoor meeting."

Carrie and Russell Peebles were members of the Human Relations Council of Grosse Pointe that invited King. According to the *Detroit News* on January 20, 1999, Russell said, "It was a very snowy, blustery night, but the auditorium was filled to capacity, about 3,000 people. The followers of Mr. Donald Lobsinger (a right-wing activist group known as Breakthrough) tried to disrupt the occasion by shouting various remarks. There were fears of violence. So, the Grosse Pointe Farms chief of police had picked up Dr. King at the airport in his own car."

In 1973, Lobsinger and Breakthrough members attacked a Catholic priest, Father Thomas Hinsberg, during a peace vigil held on the front steps of the Blessed Sacrament Cathedral. Lobsinger yelled "Judas" and "traitor" as he knocked the priest to the ground and beat him up. He and the others were arrested for disorderly conduct.

Breakthrough went on into the early 1990s and then broke up. Lobsinger lost his job with the city (which seemed amazingly tolerant of him). When asked about Lobsinger, his boss simply said, "He did his job. That was it." He moved out of Detroit to St. Clair Shores. In 1994, the Republican Party denounced him as too fanatic. He continued to speak before the city council about Communism on a regular basis.

In 2011, when a commissioner invited a Muslim imam to deliver the invocation at a board of commissioners meeting, Donald Lobsinger was there. According to the *Macomb Daily* on January 22, 2011, "Minutes after [the imam] performed the duty, longtime political rabble rouser Don Lobsinger spoke during public participation, denouncing the Martin Luther King holiday, as he does every year, and claiming that King was a Communist. Then he turned his sights on Elturk, essentially asserting that Muslim beliefs are a crime against God and the imam will be going to hell. So much for that civil tone in our politics that the President and Congress have been preaching."

Lobsinger never married. "Marriage was for raising children," he said and added that he never had the time. He never owned a house. Before he retired, he shared a flat with his father, and then he moved to a one-room apartment in St. Clair Shores with a crucifix, a print of the Last Supper and only a couple of European drinking mugs for decoration. He loved hockey and once got to scrimmage with Gordie Howe and Ted Lindsay.

As Neal Rubin described Lobsinger in a feature from June 3, 1996, when Lobsinger was sixty-one years old, "He typically saves his emotion for his work. Tall and grandfatherly with his gray hair swept up in front he looks a bit like Fred MacMurray. Then a topic sets him off and his jaw clenches, and his pointed finger trembles, and he looks like someone else entirely."

In 2018, Donald Lobsinger died.

So, here's what we were confronted with, my organization: if you don't oppose the anti-war protestors, it looks as though there's no opposition against them. If you do oppose them, the press makes you the villain. So, either way, the communists win.
—Donald Lobsinger

BIBLIOGRAPHY

This book relied on numerous articles from the *Detroit Free Press* that were too numerous to cite, along with a smattering of articles from the *New York Times*, *Wall Street Journal* and *Washington Post*. All other sources are cited below.

Ahmad, Muhammad. "The League of Revolutionary Black Workers: A Historical Study." History Is a Weapon. 2005. https://www.historyisaweapon.com.

Allen, Ernie. "Dying from the Inside: The Decline of the League of Revolutionary Black Workers." Libcom.org.

Anderson, Carlotta R. *All-American Anarchist Joseph Labadie and the Labor Movement*. Detroit, MI: Wayne State University Press, 1998.

Annual report, Detroit Police Department, 1922.

"Annual report v.: ill.; 23–25." National Association for the Advancement of Colored People Main Office, 1920.

Beals, Carlton. *Brass-Knuckle Crusade: The Great Know-Nothing Conspiracy, 1820–1860*. New York: Hastings House, 1960.

Beattie, Joseph. *The Franklin Scene: An Informal History of Detroit's Oldest Social Settlement*. Detroit, MI: N.p., 1948.

"Brinks Truck Dynamited." *Life Magazine*, June 6, 1945.

Bullock, Henry Allen. *The Role of the Negro Church in the Negro Community of Detroit*. Ann Arbor: University of Michigan, 1935.

Cochran, William Cox. "The Dream of a Northwestern Confederacy." Madison, WI: N.p., 1916.

Communism in the Detroit Area: Hearings before the United States House Committee on Un-American Activities, 82nd Cong. (1952).

Couzens, James. *Story of the Detroit Police Department, 1916–17*. Detroit, MI: Inland Press, 1917.

Crissey, Forest. *The Romance of Moving Money: Celebrating the Seventy-Fifth Anniversary of Brink's Service, 1859–1934*. Chicago: Library of Institutional Biography, 1934.

The Cyclopedia of Fraternities, a Compilation of Existing Authentic Information and the Results of Original Investigation as to More Than Six Hundred Secret Societies in the United States. New York: E.B. Treat, 1907. Reprinted Detroit, MI: Gale Research, 1966.

Darden, Joe T. *Detroit Race Riots, Racial Conflicts, and Efforts to Bridge the Racial Divide*. East Lansing: Michigan State University Press, 2013.

Dent, John Charles. *The Story of the Upper Canadian Rebellion, Largely Derived from Original Sources and Documents*. Toronto, ON: C.B. Robinson, 1885.

Desmond, Humphry J. *The A.P.A. Movement: A Sketch*. Washington, D.C.: New Century Press, 1912.

———. *The Know-Nothing Party: A Sketch*. Washington, D.C.: New Century Press, 1905.

Donald Lobsinger interview, Detroit 67, Looking Back to Move Forward, Detroit Historical Society, June 23, 2016.

"Extent of Subversion in the 'New Left': Testimony of Robert J. Thomas [and Others] Hearings, Ninety-First Congress, Second Session." Washington, D.C: U.S. Government Printing Office, 1970–71.

Fine, Sidney. *Violence in the Model City*. East Lansing: Michigan State University Press, 2007.

Frost, Julieanna. "The Rise and Fall of Michael Mills and the Detroit Jezreelites." *American Communal Societies Quarterly* 8, no. 3 (July 2014): 146–62.

Georgakas, Dan, and Marvin Surkin. *Detroit: I Do Mind Dying, A Study in Urban Revolution*. Chicago: Haymarket Books, 1998.

Geschwender, James A. *Class, Race, and Worker Insurgency*. Cambridge, UK: Cambridge University Press, 1977.

Gibson, Guy James. "Lincoln's League: The Union League Movement during the Civil War." PhD diss., University of Illinois, 1957.

Glaberman, Martin. "Black Cats, White Cats, Wildcats: Auto Workers in Detroit." *Speak Out*, 1969.

Goldberg, David. "General Baker Spent His Life in Struggle on the Streets and in the Auto Plants of Detroit." *Jacobin*, 2014.

Grimes, Warren. "The Proletarian Party in America." Department of Justice, FBI investigative file, July 20, 1921.

Hamilton, George. *House of Masses Trial- Socialist Versus Communist*. Detroit, MI: Masses Publishing House, 1921.

Hamilton, James Cleland. *John Brown in Canada*. Toronto, ON: N.p., 1894.

Hinton, Richard J. *John Brown and His Men; With Some Account of the Roads They Travelled to Reach Harper's Ferry*. New York: Funk and Wagnalls, 1894.

Hoersten, Greg. "Trying to Stamp Out Black Legion." *Lima News*, July 16, 2019.

Hutchinson, E. *Startling Facts for Native Americans Called "Know-Nothings," or, A Vivid Presentation of the Dangers to American Liberty, to Be Apprehended from Foreign Influence*. New York: E. Hutchinson, 1855.

Interview with Arnie Bernstein on WKAR-PBS, October 10, 2013.

Jackson, Kenneth T. *The Ku Klux Klan in the City 1915–1930*. New York: Oxford University Press, 1967.

Johnson, Oakley C. *Marxism in the United States History Before the Russian Revolution (1876–1917)*. New York: Humanities Press, 1974.

Kavieff, Paul. *The Purple Gang Organized Crime in Detroit 1910–1946*. New Jersey: Barricade Books, 2013.

Kilar, Jeremy W. *Germans in Michigan*. East Lansing: Michigan State University Press, 2002.

Kinchen, Oscar Arvle. *The Rise and Fall of the Patriot Hunters*. New York: Bookman Associates, 1956.

Klement, Frank L. *Dark Lanterns, Secret Political Societies, Conspiracies and Treason Trials in the Civil War*. Baton Rouge: Louisiana State University Press, 1984.

Leische, Margit. *Lipstick and Lies*. Scottsdale, AZ: Poisoned Pen Press, 2009.

Lichtenstein, Nelson, and Stephen Meyer. "On the Line, Essays in the History of Auto Work." Urbana, IL: University of Illinois Press, 1989.

Lobsinger, Donald J. Detroit, 1571028, U.S. Department of Justice, FBI, investigative file, released in 2002.

Los Angeles Times. November 21, 1925.

———. November 3, 1890.

Lumpkin, Katherine DuPre. "The General Plan Was Freedom: A Negro Secret Order on the Underground Railroad." *Phylon* 28, no. 1 (1967): 63–77.

MacDonald, Carlos Frederick, and Edward Anthony Spitzka. "The Trial, Execution, Autopsy and Mental Status of Leon F. Czolgosz, Alias Fred Nieman, the Assassin of President McKinley." N.p, 1902.

Maransis, David. "A Good American Family." New York: Simon and Schuster, 2019.

Maynard, Mark. "Exploring Ypsilanti's Place on the Underground Railroad: Part One." *Mark Maynard* (blog), November 30, 2014. http://markmaynard.com.

———. "Exploring Ypsilanti's Place on the Underground Railroad: Part Two." *Mark Maynard* (blog), January 7, 2015. http://markmaynard.com.

Michigan Historical Collections. V.12, 1887.

Michigan Historical Collections. V.21, 1894.

Morris, George. "The Black Legion Rides." New York: Workers Library Publishers, 1936.

Mugan, Monica. "The Hapless Hero Who 'Saved' Upper Canada." *MacCleans*, October 16, 1965.

Plummer, Kevin. "Historicist: Socialite and Nazi Spy Toronto's Grace Buchanan-Dineen's Life of Intrigue and Espionage in Detroit." *Torontoist*, April 1, 2017.

Rankin, Louis. *Detroit Nationality Groups*. Lansing: Michigan Historical Commission, 1939.

Ross, Robert Budd. "The Patriot War." N.p: 1890.

Rubin, Neal. "He'd Rather Be Right." *Detroit Free Press*, June 3, 1996.

Russo, Linda. "Underground Railroad; United States Department of the Interior, National Park Service." U.S. Department of the Interior, National Park Service, Denver Service Center, 1995.

Sase, John, and Jerald Senick. "The Odd and Curious Case of Max Stephan Part 2." *Detroit Legal News*, May 15, 2013.

Senick, Jerald. "The Odd and Curious Case of Max Stephan." *Detroit Legal News*, April 17, 2013.

Siebert, Wilbur Henry. *The Underground Railroad, from Slavery to Freedom*. New York: Macmillan, 1898.

Smith, J. Fairbairn, and Charles Fey. "History of Freemasonry in Michigan." Vol. 1 and 2. Fort Worth: Grand Lodge Free and Accepted Masons of Michigan, 1963.

Southern Workman, 1923.

Stanton, Tom. *Terror in the City of Champions, Murder, Baseball and the Secret Society that Shocked Depression-Era Detroit*. Guilford, CT: Lyons Press, 2016.

Stevens, Albert Clark. *The Cyclopaedia of Fraternities*. Detroit, MI: Gale Research Co., 1966.

Stoddard, William Osborn. *Lincoln's Third Secretary: The Memoirs of Willian O. Stoddard*. Edited with an introduction by William O. Stoddard Jr. and a foreword by Edgar De Witt Jones. New York: Exposition Press, 1955.

Sugrue, Thomas J. "Driving While Black: The Car and Race Relations in Modern America." *Automobiles in American Life and Society*, 2010.

Thomas, Sister M. Evangeline. "Nativism in the Old Northwest, 1850–1860." PhD thesis, Catholic University of America, 1936.

Tiffany, Orrin Edward. *The Relations of the United States to the Canadian Rebellion of 1837–1838*. Ann Arbor: University of Michigan, 1905.

Van Ells, Mark D. "Americans For Hitler—the Bund." America in World War II. http://www.americainwwii.com.

Vinyard, JoEllen McNergney. *Right in Michigan's Grassroots*. Ann Arbor: University of Michigan Press, 2013.

Vismara, John C. "The Coming of Italians to Detroit." *Michigan History Magazine*, 1918.

Washington, Forrest B. "The Negro in Detroit: A Survey of the Conditions of a Negro Group in a Northern Industrial Center During the War Prosperity Period." Associated Charities of Detroit, Research Bureau, 1920.

White, Frank Marshall. "The Passing of the Black Hand." *New Century Magazine*, 1917.

"White in Candidate." *Metrotimes*, July 5, 2006.

Widick, B.J. "Detroit City of Race and Class Violence." Detroit, MI: Wayne State University Press, 1989.

Wolcott, Victoria W. "Mediums, Messages, and Lucky Numbers: African-American Female Spiritualists and Numbers Runner in Interwar Detroit," in *The Geography of Identity*. Ann Arbor: University of Michigan Press, 1999.

Woodford, Frank. *Father Abraham's Children: Michigan Episodes in the Civil War*. Detroit, MI: Wayne State University Press, 1961.

Work Stoppages: Motor Vehicles, and Motor Vehicle Equipment Industry, 1927–58. Washington, D.C.: U.S. Bureau of Labor Statistics, 1959.

ABOUT THE AUTHOR

Motor City native Bill Loomis is the author of *Detroit's Delectable Past*, *Detroit Food* and *On This Day in Detroit History*, as well as numerous articles for the *Detroit News*, *Michigan History Magazine*, *Hour Detroit*, *Crains Business Detroit* and a variety of national media, including the *New York Times*. He has been interviewed on the PBS radio show *Splendid Table* and was a regular contributor to *Stateside with Cynthia Canty* on PBS-WUOM in Ann Arbor. He also appears regularly on Detroit talk shows and history-based shows like *Mysteries at the Museum*. He lives in Ann Arbor.